Pevensey C̲a̲

A Handbook for Teachers
Dot Meades

CONTENTS

English Heritage

Teachers' notes

The pack is designed to provide two complete schemes of work for class visits to the site: one for the Roman fort, one for the medieval castle. There is thus material for two possible 'ready made' visits with classroom follow-up activities closely linked to the visit.

Various adaptations may be desirable if a particular theme is being followed, to suit the abilities of particular groups of children, or to make the best use of a short visit. It is hoped that the information and ideas provided in the book will make the task of adaptation easier.

For example, teachers of classes that are following a Roman theme will want to spend most of their visit looking at the detail of the Roman fort but, particularly if they have come a long distance they may also wish to take the opportunity of seeing the medieval castle. The teacher can use the medieval Activity Sheets to pre-select points of comparison with the Roman fort, e.g. building materials, size, fortification, without requiring the children to complete those sheets.

If a medieval theme is being followed, but emphasis is to be more on fortification than on living conditions, the children could start with the Roman Activity Sheet no. 1 and do less of Medieval Activity Sheet no. 3. If the opposite is the case, then Medieval Activity Sheet no. 4 will become the focus, with perhaps extra tasks being added by the teacher and role play emphasised.

Young children will need much less to do, and some of the questions should be omitted, the teacher or helper can point out the features they cover and answer any queries the children may ask.

Preparation for the visit

Checklist

1. Read through the hand book.
2. Book your visit (see address at the end of this handbook).
3. If possible, make your own preliminary visit to the castle.
4. Book transport.
5. Enlist adult helpers and provide them with relevant Teachers' notes and other information.
6. Adapt the Activity Sheets to the needs of your class.
7. Prepare and teach preliminary lessons (see suggestions below).
8. Decide what groups the children will work in at the site.
9. Duplicate Activity Sheets. (First check whether Sheets are to be used by class or group as this will affect the numbers required).
10. Assemble other equipment needed for the visit, i.e. pencils, spare paper, rulers, measuring tapes, clip boards etc.

You may photocopy the plans and activities in this book for work on-site or in the classroom.

Suggestions for pre-visit work

1. Locate Roman/Norman/Medieval/ Tudor/Second World War in time, perhaps by means of a Time Line (see end of these notes for relevant dates). Useful historical 'pegs' for each period might be: Roman invasion, the building of Anderita, Saxon sacking of Anderita, Norman invasion, Battle of Lewes, Spanish Armada, countries involved in Second World War. (See Histories of the fort and the castle).
2. Locate Pevensey geographically, particularly in relation to the changing shoreline and Pevensey Rape. (See The Landscape).
3. Use illustrative material on dress, ways of life, weapons and castles. (See Bibliography but there are many other excellent publications. A selection of books can usually be provided by the schools library service where this exists).
4. Introduce words which appear on the Activity Sheets but which children may not know, e.g. bastion, towers, curtain wall, etc. (See Glossary).

---

5. Practise measuring, using ruler, measuring tape or other methods.
6. Relate what the children will see on their visit to other evidence in their locality which belongs to the same period, e.g. other castles, churches, houses and artifacts in museums. This will help the children to base imagination on fact, an important historical and archaeological skill.

After the visit

Go through the children's answers to the on-site questions with the whole class, making sure that they have grasped the most important points. Each group should have the opportunity to pass on their particular findings to others who did not cover the same ground, either verbally or by taking part in some co-operative project such as the making of a model, frieze or wall-chart.

Adapt follow-up Activity Sheets as necessary and teach the techniques of scale drawing or enlarging a drawing if these are needed. Some follow-up tasks require the use of additional illustrative material or information and relevant books should be available for children to use.

BELOW: The moat and Gatehouse.

English Heritage

Introduction

By their nature, castles had to be strongly built and because of their strength they are among the few really ancient buildings to have survived in recognisable form. A visit to any castle provides fascinating glimpses into the past but the visitor to Pevensey is doubly fortunate because there are, in fact, two fortifications: a Roman fort and a medieval castle. The first, and outer, fort was built in about AD 340; the second was begun in early Norman times and has been added to over the centuries. The last additions were made during The Second World War.

This long period of repeated development, desertion and reoccupation makes Pevensey a particularly valuable castle for school visits. It means that it can be a focus point for a study of Roman, Norman, medieval or later periods, or it can be used to show the development of castle design in response to changes in weaponry.

Pevensey has also much to offer in terms of its situation. Within the fort, there is ample space for school parties to work individually or in groups. Measuring, simple surveying and other work can be carried on without inconveniencing other visitors. There is plenty of room for picknicking and it is easy for coaches to drop their passengers in a quiet road by the Roman West Gate.

Many writers on local history comment on a general lack of awareness of the evidence of the past which surrounds us. History in the abstract is a difficult study for children and one way to get over this difficulty is to reach their minds in a more concrete way through archaeology. Since archaeology is the study of the visible remains of the past, what better introduction could there be than a visit to Pevensey, which has stood for so many centuries and reflects so much of our national history.

To help pupils to get the most out of a visit, preliminary lessons will be necessary. They will need to know essential background information and to practise measuring and other skills for their on-site activities. They will enjoy their visit more if, in their imagination, they can 'people' the castle and try to reconstruct the way the inhabitants lived, what the problems of defence were, and so on. The preliminary study of illustrative material is very important.

A visit to Pevensey Castle sites can provide an excellent focus for integrating the skills normally associated with separate subjects, such as mathematics — measuring, simple surveying, calculation of time and distance, angles and height. Geography and geology can be considered in relation to the situation of the site and the use of various building materials. The changing shoreline is a problem that is still with us. The archaeological and historical aspects can be shown to be integrated. Creative writing, art, drama and role-play can be either factually or imaginatively based — ideally both should be encouraged.

It is hoped that teachers will find enough information in this hand book to stimulate their own interest as well as providing material for interesting lessons. The Activity Sheets give opportunities for children to work as a class, in groups and individually at the site and afterwards, and to share the knowledge they have gained with other groups. The hand book is aimed at a fairly wide age range and no doubt adaptations will be needed to fit the needs of certain classes or individual children. The aim of the hand book has been to help teachers to give the children as varied an experience of the fort and castle as possible and to suggest follow-up activities that make use of and enhance that experience. For this reason, the tasks set on follow-up Activity Sheets are closely related to those on the on-site Activity Sheets and any adaptations will need to take this into account.

The thirteenth century Gatehouse.

Pevensey coastline c. A.D. 340 — Estuary, Harbour, Roman road, West Gate, Postern, Roman fort, East Gate, Open sea, Harbour. N. 200 metres

The Landscape

Anderita was the name the Romans gave to their fort which was built at the place we now call Pevensey, in about AD 340. The fort now stands on dry land about a mile from today's Channel coastline which, however, has considerably altered since Roman times.

In those days, Pevensey was a peninsula forming the westernmost point of an area of land which jutted out into a large inlet. This inlet had its entrance from the open sea between what is now Eastbourne and Cooden. The sites of present-day Wartling, Herstmonceux, Magham Down and Hailsham, now far inland, were within a mile of its coast. It was sheltered from the prevailing south-westerly winds by the South Downs and Beachy Head.

Within the inlet were other areas of higher ground, including the sites of present-day Horseye, Rickney, Chilley and Northeye, whose names indicate that they were once marshy islands. The River Ashbourne entered it from the north and numerous small rivers and streams also drained into it, bringing silt washed down from the mainland. Even in those days, there must have been extensive areas of silty marshland, flooded with salt water at high tide.

Pevensey itself was joined to the mainland by a narrow neck of dry land leading westwards to Stone Cross and Polegate. There was water deep enough on the east and north of the peninsula to shelter Roman merchant ships and war

3

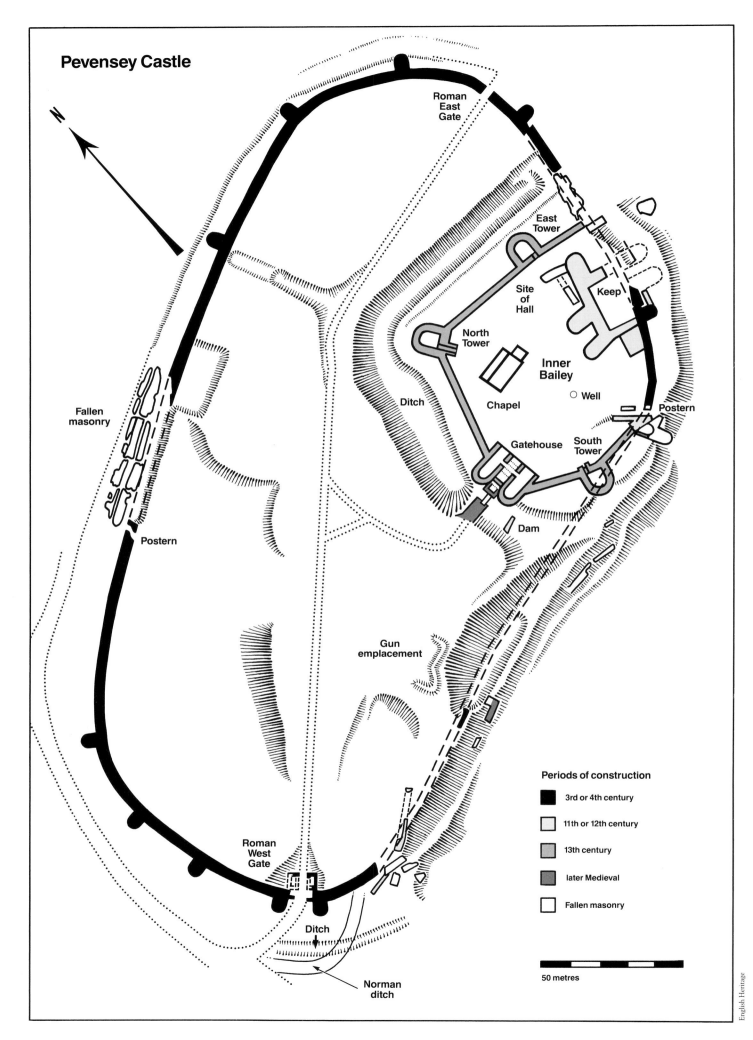

Pevensey Castle

N

Roman East Gate

East Tower

Site of Hall

Keep

North Tower

Inner Bailey

○ Well

Chapel

Ditch

Postern

Gatehouse

South Tower

Dam

Fallen masonry

Postern

Gun emplacement

Roman West Gate

Ditch

Norman ditch

Periods of construction

- 3rd or 4th century
- 11th or 12th century
- 13th century
- later Medieval
- Fallen masonry

50 metres

English Heritage

Aerial view from the south west.

galleys. Archaeological excavation has shown that a ditch 5.5m wide was dug across the isthmus of dry land thereby effectively turning Anderita into an island fortress.

When the Normans arrived to invade Britain in AD 1066, the area was still a mixture of sea and marsh and the main rivers were still navigable. A small settlement had grown up on dry land to the east of the Roman fortifications. With the building of a Norman castle in the south-eastern corner of the Roman fort, this settlement increased and became a small but thriving port. In the meantime, the land around the inlet was settled and farmed. Farmers found that their animals did well on the salt-marsh, although sometimes they were lost when the marsh flooded during violent storms. Over the centuries, the marsh was enclosed, reclaimed and drained. Natural silting and the eastward movement of shingle along the coast, added to this deliberate reclamation, ensured that eventually the whole of the inlet became dry land.

From at least the fourteenth century, when silting became a real problem, efforts were made to keep the port of Pevensey open by means of cuts and sluices to the sea. These efforts were of no permanent use and by the mid-seventeenth century Pevensey was landlocked.

The marsh is still scored by deep ditches, the most notable of which runs beside the road leading to Pevensey Bay. Historical geographers have traced the remnants of successive sea walls and banks which were built to protect the 'new' land as the sea receded.

The recession of the sea not only meant the end of Pevensey as a port but it was also a contributory cause in making the castle obsolescent as a means of coastal defence. Not until the twentieth century did its geographical position become once again of strategic significance.

Archaeological excavations in the Roman fort have indicated that underlying the topsoil there is a bed of clay (in one place slightly less than 4m deep) and beneath the clay, a vein of sand. There is evidence that both of these materials were dug out from the area of the Roman fort. This digging took place at the time when the Roman fort was built and also later when the Norman castle was being rebuilt in stone.

Anderita
Historical background

For most of the first and second centuries after the Roman Conquest, the area that we now call Sussex was a peaceful and prosperous part of the Empire. Leading British families were encouraged to adopt the Roman way of life and to co-operate with, or even become, Roman officials. Villas were established, the iron industry greatly expanded, agriculture and trade flourished. Romano-British communities used vast quantities of pottery, the everyday (usually called coarser) wares being locally made, the finer ones usually imported. Fishbourne Palace and villas such as those at Bignor and Preston Park must have been richly furnished in keeping with their owners' high status.

Such prosperity had its dangers, however, for later it attracted attacks from Saxon raiders intent on plunder, which gradually increased to the point where more fortifications were needed to defend the coastal areas. The eastern coasts of Britain were the first to be attacked and between AD 220 and 230 this prompted the building of two forts, the first of a series which eventually became known as the 'Saxon Shore Forts.' These two were Brancaster, built to protect the Wash and Reculver to safeguard the Thames Estuary. They supplemented the one at Dover where the Roman fleet was based.

Between AD 270 and 285, in response to continued attacks, the main series of the Saxon Shore forts was constructed.

In an effort to achieve a permanent solution to the problem, the central government in Rome appointed Carausius, a successful Belgian commander and sailor 'to rid the seas of Belgica and Armorica of pirates.' (That is, all along the Gallic channel coast line). By the mid 280s Carausius controlled both sides of the

Channel and saw his chance to acquire even greater power. He broke with the central government and set himself up as a Roman emperor, based on Britain and the coastal regions of Gaul.

There are conflicting reports about his 'reign'. He was said to have made wise financial reforms but his enemies accused him of allowing raids to take place and then intercepting the pirates at sea to obtain a share of the loot. His powerful navy certainly contained a considerable number of barbarians.

Not surprisingly, the Emperor Maximian, in charge of the Western Empire, objected to Carausius' claim on his territory but there was little he could do. After winning a decisive battle at sea, Carausius remained in power until AD 293, when a determined effort by Constantius, backed by the Emperor Diocletian, resulted in the capture of Carausius' main base at Boulogne. Carausius was promptly murdered by his finance minister, Allectus, who succeeded him. Three years later, Constantius attacked Britain with two invasion forces, one of which landed near Southampton to march inland towards London, the other went directly to London by sea. Allectus attacked the inland force but was defeated and killed at a battle somewhere in north Hampshire. The remnants of his army included mercenary soldiers, who marched on London, presumably with the idea of looting the town. Constantius' sea-borne force reached London first and were thankfully welcomed by the Londoners. As was the Roman habit, a coin was struck to commemorate this important event and to publicise it. Peace and prosperity were restored to Britain, at least for the time being. Archaeological evidence from Portchester shows that the Romans took the precaution of de-militarising the fort and for some years it was occupied only by a civilian community. The last Saxon Shore fort had yet to be built.

In AD 337 the Emperor Constantius I died. Five years later, in AD 342 the new

The insignia of the *Comes Litoris Saxonici per Britannias* from the Oxford *Notitia* manuscript.

Emperor Constans visited Britain in mid-winter. There must have been a serious crisis to bring him across the Channel at that time of year and this is borne out by archaeological evidence, which shows that the forts were cleared of their civilian communities and that soldiers were re-installed. A new command was set up to guard the southern and eastern coasts under the direction of its commander the 'Count of the Saxon Shore.' The *Notitia Dignitatum,* an official handbook of the civil and military organization of the late Roman Empire, lists the troops and the forts commanded by the Count.

There were nine coastal forts, protecting the coast between Portchester and Brancaster. The list includes the last one to be built, Anderita. It tells us that for twenty five years Anderita was the base of the *Numerus Albucorum,* an auxiliary unit of irregular troops from the Belgian tribe of the Albucii. It does not tell us the date when the fort was built. However, during an archaeological excavation, a coin dated AD 330-335 found beneath one of the bastions suggests that the fort was built after that time. A large number of coins of the 340s confirms that the fort was occupied then. As a result of these finds it is now thought that the fort was constructed about AD 340. Excavation also revealed tiled hearths regularly spaced about 5.5m apart, suggesting barrack-like buildings, perhaps to house workmen or troops, coin evidence again suggesting occupation during the 340s.

However, the Saxon Shore forts and even Hadrian's Wall could not save the Romano-British population from the disaster of AD 367. The historian Ammianus tells us that in this year there was a great 'barbarian conspiracy.' In the north, Hadrian's Wall was completely overrun, in spite of being fully garrisoned. The Count of the Saxon Shore was killed and the military leader of Roman Britain

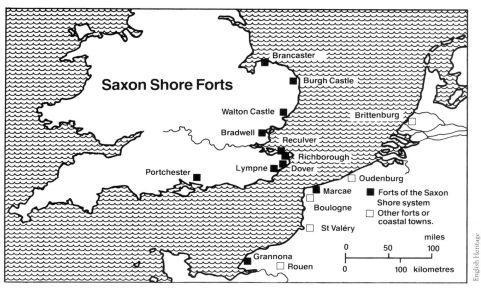

was captured. Large numbers of military deserters and escaped slaves roamed the country, looting and plundering. This state of affairs continued for a year until Count Theodosius landed at Richborough with four regiments of the field army and began to re-establish order.

He offered a general amnesty to deserters. Rebels and invaders were gradually cleared from Britain and Theodosius set about reorganising the frontiers. Coin evidence shows that Anderita was maintained as a strong point into the fifth century.

It seems likely that in these troubled times, many of the wealthier people left their country estates to live more securely in the towns. Chichester added bastions to the city wall and re-cut its defensive ditch. It may have had a small defensive militia. Hill-forts were re-fortified: Highdown, which is near the sea and which archaeological evidence has shown was occupied in the fourth-century, may have acted as another strong point. For about twenty years, the Romano-British managed to maintain some sort of civilised existence but other factors were to lead to their downfall.

Between AD 383 and 407, armies were drawn from Britain to fight on the continent, ostensibly to protect Britain but often in reality to support the ambitions of their commanders. They were beaten and very few returned. Central government in Rome was not interested in losers and had little sympathy for the troubles which arose in Britain as a consequence of this serious loss of manpower. After the last army left in AD 407, Britain was virtually defenceless. The historian Zosimus described how, in AD 410, the British communities responded to severe Saxon attacks.

'The Britons took up arms, and braving danger for their own independence, freed their cities from the barbarians threatening them: and all Armorica and the other provinces of Gaul copied the British example and freed themselves in the same way, expelling their Roman governors and establishing a state of their own as best they could.'

Britain had, apparently, appealed to the Emperor Honorius for help but he sent back a message telling them to 'look after their own defence.'

It seems likely that each city defended itself and its locality and would have had its own leaders. Gildas records that in about AD 430 Vortigern was the overall British leader. Since they were still troubled by Saxon attacks, Vortigern decided to follow the Roman practice of employing barbarian mercenary soldiers to protect them. Archaeological evidence suggests that these mercenary bands may have been given their own distinct territories. Professor Cunliffe, in his book *The Regni*, suggests that there were in this area six different districts, three British based on Anderita, Chichester and possibly Hassocks; and three Saxon based on or near Portchester, Highdown and Alfriston/Bishopstone where

CARAUSIUS (286-93) *The obverse of this silver coin shows the Emperor. His name is given after the letters* IMP — *an abbreviation of* IMPERATOR *or Emperor.*

The reverse shows Britannia clasping the hand of the Emperor and the words EXPECTATE VENI — *'come, our long-awaited hope'. Emperors often used coins to make propaganda points.*

ALLECTUS (293-6) *was the finance minister of Carausius, whom he murdered to become emperor.*

CONSTANTIUS I (293-306). *He overthrew the usurper in Britain, Allectus. Constantius struck this gold medallion to celebrate the victory. He died in York and was succeeded by his son Constantine (the Great).*

CONSTANS (337-50) *was one of the sons of the Emperor Constantine the Great. The reverse of this coin (not shown here) has a phoenix and the words* FEL TEMP REPARATIO — *'Happy days are here again'.*

archaeological finds suggest early and well-established 'Germanic settlement.'

This policy worked for a time but in AD 442, the mercenaries claimed that they were not being paid well enough. They moved out of their territories and overran the country, Gildas says, 'until destroying the neighbouring towns and lands (they) reached the other side of the island and dippled (their) red and savage tongue in the Western Ocean.' There is a famous message which was sent to the Roman general Aetius in Gaul, 'The barbarians drive us to the sea, the sea drives us to the barbarians. Between the two means of death we are either killed or drowned.' No help came from Aetius. The Gallic Chronicle tells us that in the year AD 442, 'Britain long troubled by various happenings and disasters passed under the authority of the Saxons.'

The Anglo-Saxon Chronicle briefly describes three Saxon attacks which seem to have brought about the final downfall of the British communities. In AD 477 they landed at a place called Cymens-ora, which a later charter suggests was on the coast south of Chichester. In AD 485, Aella fought the Britons on the bank of a river called Mearcradburn. This name probably means 'the river of the frontier agreed by treaty.' This may either be the present-day Ouse or the Adur which, according to modern theory, were possible boundaries of another remaining British area. Finally, what seems to have been the most savage attack of all took place at Andredscester, identified as Anderita, which we know now as Pevensey. The Anglo-Saxon Chronicle states the facts quite baldly, AD 491.

'In this year Aella and Cissa besieged Andredesceaster and slew all the inhabitants; there was not even one Briton left there.'

Henry of Huntingdon, writing in the 12th century gives us a fuller account, perhaps compiled from documents which are no longer available, perhaps partly from imagination or from stories handed down by word of mouth,

"Aella besieged Andredcester, a strongly fortified city. The Britons then collected like bees and beat the besiegers in the day by strategems and in the night by attacks. No day, no night occurred when unfavourable and fresh tidings would not exasperate the minds of the Saxons; but, rendered more ardent, they beset the city with continual assaults. Always, however, as they might assail, the Britons pressed them behind with archers and with darts thrown from thongs. . . The Saxons were long annoyed and an immense slaughter of them was made. . . But the citizens, worn down by long want of food, when they could no longer sustain the multitude of assailants, were all devoured of the sword, with the women and little ones, so that no individual escaped."

During an archaeological excavation in the Roman fort at Pevensey, spear, javelin and arrow heads and *"small iron objects pointed at each end"* were found at a level which was laid down at the end of the Romano-British period. Dr. Salzmann speculated that the 'small iron objects' may have been tips for darts and the level indicates that they could belong to the time of this last Saxon siege.

The lack of British place-names in the area has given rise to the theory that the Saxons killed or drove out all the remaining Britons that had lived there. The place that had been Anderita eventually acquired a new name, of Saxon origin — Pevensey.

The Garrison and the Britons

For 25 years the fort was garrisoned by soldiers from Belgium who belonged to a tribe called the Abulcii. They were not Roman legionaries but 'irregular' soldiers who fought for the Romans and were paid by them. There may have been up to a thousand of these soldiers at Anderita.

The fact that these soldiers came from Belgium probably did not seem as strange to the local Britons as it would to us nowadays, because both peoples belonged to the Roman Empire. If they were in the army, they knew they could be posted to any part of the Empire where they might be needed. Probably their languages were very similar because they may well have had ancestors in common.

Living Quarters

Soldiers usually lived in barracks, long buildings divided into rooms, each with a hearth where they could have a fire. Archaeological evidence from Anderita suggests that these hearths were about 5.48m apart and that the walls of the barracks were made of wattle and daub and the roofs were thatched.

Although several excavations have taken place in the fort, no remains of any stone buildings have been found. It seems likely that there would have been at least one good house for the commander but this may have been made out of wood. Its remains may lie in a part of the fort that has not been examined, perhaps even under the medieval castle.

So we have to look at pictures of other Roman buildings and try to imagine what those in the fort might have been like. In doing so, it must be remembered that by the time Anderita was built, Roman civilization in Britain was past its best, so very elaborate buildings in the fort were unlikely.

Apart from housing, there must have been pens for the domestic animals and workshops for the craftsmen who maintained the fort and produced goods for everyday use. Slaves and free workpeople would all have needed shelter either inside the fort or in a settlement outside its walls.

The Lunt Roman Fort (reconstruction), Coventry. Perhaps Pevensey had buildings of wood like this.

City of Coventry Museums

Work — Soldiers and Sailors

The soldiers based at the fort would have spent much of their time training. Roman war galleys based at Anderita regularly patrolled the coast and the Channel to drive away Saxon pirates and invaders. Some soldiers would have been carried in the galleys to help in any hand-to-hand fighting that might take place. No doubt there would also have been regular patrols inland to make sure that no Saxons had landed elsewhere on the coast and to keep them from creeping up the rivers in their boats to raid inland settlements.

Roman ships would also supply the fort with anything that could not be made there, including any luxuries. During the time the fort was being built they probably brought in stone, and other building materials.

Work — Craftsmen and others

Potters and their assistants dug and prepared clay, worked it either by hand (for very large pots) or using a potter's wheel, built and tended their kilns, loaded and unloaded their pots.

Leatherworkers converted the skins of animals into leather, then made the leather into boots, shoes and sandals for the people, horse saddles and harness, water bottles and other articles.

Carpenters would always be busy, maintaining the buildings and repairing damage to ships, making carts and waggons and mending or replacing their wheels as well as providing simple furniture, and anything else made of wood.

Blacksmiths also made and repaired tools, made rims for the wooden wheels, nails for the buildings, and so on.

Slaves helped with all the less skilled jobs and this would have included keeping the fort clean and tidy, loading and unloading ships, tending animals and waiting on the more important people. However, if a slave had some useful skill, like carpentry, he would be put to work in this way and some of the best craftsmen were slaves. If a slave did particularly well, he might be given his freedom.

Food

Remains found by archaeologists tell us a great deal about what the people ate in those days. The bones of oxen, sheep, deer, pigs and wild boar have been found, so we know that they ate meat from these animals. The oxen, sheep and pigs would have been kept on or near the fort and the wild animals were probably hunted by the local people and sold to those in the fort. Fish probably formed a large part of their diet, as they were so near the sea. Certainly, large quantities of shellfish were eaten — heaps of their shells have been found by archaeologists. Cockles and mussels seem to have been particular favourites.

Bird bones, too, have been found: chickens, grey geese and other wild birds were probably eaten.

We know from the discovery of a quern that they ground corn to make flour. The corn would probably have been grown on the nearby South Downs and when the fort was fully garrisoned they must have needed very large quantities to feed them all. It would have been brought into the fort either by sea, possibly landing at the East Gate, or by waggons coming by road, over the bridge and into the West Gate. Once in the fort, slaves would unload it and store it in barns.

Description of the fort

Early Roman forts were semi-permanent, elaborate constructions with two ditches, gates, palisade, and rampart towers made of wood. Once they had conquered most of Britain, they built more permanent castles in stone but still of a similar pattern. Like the early ones, these forts were usually square or 'playing card' shape, with large gates set in the middle of each side, so that troops could come out of the fort quickly to deal with any trouble. They built a string of such forts along Hadrian's wall to keep out the Picts. The Romans did not expect to fight from these forts; they were confident enough to come out of them and fight an attacker in the open.

Towards the end of the Roman period, however, when the Saxon shore forts were built, the basic design was modified, to give them the best defence against possibly superior forces which they could no longer be absolutely sure of beating in the open. Anderita is a good example. The walls are entirely made of stone and rubble, more than 3.6m thick and originally they stood about 9m high. There are only two main gates: the East Gate is narrow by Roman standards and the West Gate very heavily defended. Every part of the wall is overlooked by massive bastions designed for archery and artillery, carefully placed so that no attacker could approach the wall without coming under fire.

The site was carefully chosen, not only to guard harbours and river entrances that might otherwise have been used by their enemies as invasion routes but also to be easily defended should those enemies appear in large numbers. At the time of building, the fort must have seemed impregnable and a great comfort to the

The West Gate

Romano-British communities living nearby. And so it remained for more than a century, sustained by manpower and supplies from the countryside around it. Only when the Saxons had taken possession of that countryside and deprived those in the fort of essential supplies, were the defenders finally overcome. No castle or fort could hold out indefinitely in an enemy-occupied land.

The Roman walls enclose an oval area of a little under 4 hectares (10 acres). The longer axis of this irregular shape runs from south-west to north-east.

The West Gate and Gatehouse

Strictly, this is at the south-west of the fort, the only direction from which it could be approached by land. It is the main entrance to Anderita and was probably approached by a wooden bridge across the 5.5m ditch which separated the fort from the mainland.

Roman ditch by the West Gate.

Part of this ditch has been re-excavated and can be seen to right of the entrance. Going into the fort, the bastion on the left side still stands up to parapet level, the one on the right being rather lower.

Little can now be seen of the gatehouse which was attached to the inner walls of the bastions. However, excavated remains show that there was an arched entrance 2.7m wide, with an oblong guardhouse on each side, projecting into the fort. This gatehouse was probably two or even three storeys high and about 5.5m in length. A nineteenth century excavation found two large bases of cylindrical columns of 'whitish friable stone' but it is not known exactly where these were.

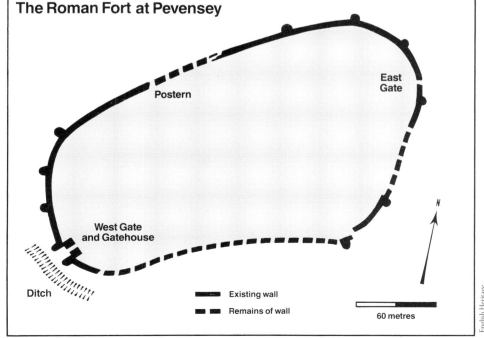

The Roman Fort at Pevensey

Postern

East Gate

West Gate and Gatehouse

Ditch

N

▬▬▬ Existing wall

▬ ▬ ▬ Remains of wall

60 metres

The East Gate, adjacent walls and Bastions

The East Gate was simply an archway. Unlike the West Gate it had no gatehouse or bastions. Excavators found traces of a wooden causeway which led from this gate to the harbour. The lack of fortification to this gate is puzzling but perhaps the builders considered that the harbour and the galleys based there were enough protection. It will be noticed that the earth inside the fort has built up over the last sixteen centuries. The original sill of the gate was found 1.5m below the present level. The gate is still the original width but was rebuilt in Norman times. The upper part of the present gate is a modern reconstruction of the Norman entrance. The floor of the gate was rough

The East Gate

Roman concrete made of flints in mortar. One odd feature, so far unexplained, is a space 1.1m wide in the centre of the gate where the concrete had been broken away.

Stones of the original arch indicate that its highest point was about 3.3m above the Roman floor level. The thickness of the wall is about 3.7m about average for the Roman walls. The walls stand on deep foundations. At the lowest level there is a 15cm layer of red clay. Above this, 90cm of flints in chalk and then 45cm of concrete made of flints in mortar. The width of the foundations corresponds to the widest part of the wall, including plinths on the outside.

The bastion to the south of the East Gate includes twentieth century alterations made early in the war of 1939-45. A bastion to the north has herring-bone repairs which have been attributed to the Normans, and the north-west bastion has another Norman addition. The bastions are solid and could have supported ballistas.

The North Postern

The remains of this small gateway can be found in the north-west wall, just south-west of the fallen part. The gate was approached by a curved passage in the wall. The gate is signposted but may be difficult for children to imagine as only the left side can really be seen. It can be identified mainly by the pattern of tile and stone. The gateway has now been filled in and there are twentieth century defences amongst the fallen masonry on its right. However, we have the evidence of an excavation to confirm that the passage enters the wall at a right-angle, then curves to the east and finally back to the west, emerging outside the fort almost at a right-angle again. The width of the inner entrance was estimated to be about double that of the outlet. This would have given the defenders of the fort an advantage, since two men fighting side by side could meet an attacker, but the enemy could only enter the passage one at a time from outside. No doubt the curving passage also made it easier to defend.

The height of this gateway was 2.1m to the turning of the arch and 3m to its highest point. Excavators also came across a possible path running from the postern up into the fort, made of beach boulders.

The Walls

The wall on the north side is in comparatively good condition and remains standing to a height of about 7.6m except for a section to the east of the north postern.

Southern (seaward) section. This wall has collapsed along most of its length but excavation has shown that remains are still there and these can be seen at various points. It appears as though a bastion may also have fallen at its western end. Also at

Second World War defences concealed in fallen Roman masonry.

this end are remains of a Norman addition to the wall and Second World War defences which have been cleverly concealed amongst the fallen Roman masonry. The destruction of the southern wall was partly due to attack by the forces of the younger Simon de Montfort in AD 1264-65 and partly due to a landslip.

From this area, the difference between the height of the land where the fort is and that of the fields where the sea used to be is very obvious.

At a point near to the line of the wall, the site of a Tudor gun emplacement is marked. It is also possible to look out towards the present-day coast and see the line of Martello Towers which were built for coastal defence during the Napoleonic wars.

Eastern/south-eastern Section. In this area, the Roman walls were incorporated into those of the later Norman/medieval castle. The medieval keep rested on one section of the Roman wall, now fallen. This section of the walls can be most clearly seen from the car park. The present car park may have been part of the harbour in Roman times. From there, it is possible to see Roman and Norman walls with Second World War additions.

BELOW: Part of the southern Roman wall. Both brick banding and putlogs can be seen clearly.

North/north-western section. The wall on this side is in comparatively good condition and remains standing to a height of over 7.6m in many places. There is one fallen section just to the east of the north postern where defences from Second World War are concealed. Although it is not possible to go through the north postern, there is a way through the collapsed section of this northern wall. This leads to a small grassy area on the *outside* of the fort, from where the outside wall can be safely viewed. From this point it is possible to study the outside wall in more or less its original condition, as most of the facing stone remains and tile courses can be clearly seen.

The inside of the wall can also be studied here, where a section of it has been cleared down to Roman level, showing the offset base of the wall.

An archaeological investigation of the wall and bastion in this area found that the lower plinth stones rest on concrete 23 to 28cm thick. Below this, there are three layers of flints in fine chalk. This rests on red clay. Where the wall descended to marsh level, extra support in the form of small stakes driven into the red clay, and timbers under the wall and bastion had been given. These timbers had completely decayed, leaving only traces in the cavities where they had once been. Concrete had been spread over and around them.

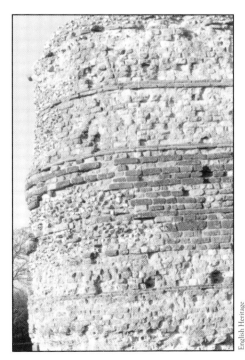

Bastion by the West Gate.

The Bastions

There were probably at least fifteen bastions built into the walls when the fort was originally constructed. Ten of these now survive. They are not all the same distance apart but have been so spaced that defenders placed upon them would have all attackers in their line of fire. For this reason they are more frequent along the walls on

the east and west sides of the fort, and less so on the straighter northern section. Presumably there were few or none on the now-fallen southern section for the same reason.

The present remains of the bastions are solid, although it has been suggested that they originally had hollow upper storeys with crenellated walls 61cm thick. These upper storeys would have provided shelter for soldiers keeping watch and might also have been used as emplacements for large weapons such as ballistas. Communications would have been via the walkway which went round the inner wall to link the bastions with each other and the main gates. The remains of crenellations which have survived are believed to be Norman, part of their re-fortification of the Roman fort.

Building methods

It is apparent from information revealed by excavation that the work of building the wall followed a set order. After initially marking out the area of the wall, work proceeded as follows:

1. A trench in the natural clay was cut to a depth of 91cm, the removed clay being thrown inwards.
2. Where the ground was marshy, oak piles were driven into the clay to help to anchor it.
3. Layers of chalk and flints were consolidated, 91cm deep and 4.6m wide. Thick planks were laid across in marshy places.
4. 23cm of concrete was laid on this.
5. The wall was partly built and faced.
6. The clay dug from the original trench was thrown back against the inner side of the wall to form a bank, making the level inside the wall 1.8m higher than the outside.
7. The wall was then completed.

The construction was 68cm thick, using a rubble core (flint, chalk, mortar) faced with greensand blocks. The walls were built by gangs of workmen, each group building a stretch 1.2 to 1.5m long. There is very obvious evidence of this in many places where the wall is breaking up into sections due to erosion and perhaps also to the drying out and shifting of the original clay base. The tile bands are usually only the depth of one tile but they had a practical use, being laid after each stage to level out irregularities in the facing blocks, to bond the blocks with the core and also to serve as a support for scaffolding from which the next stage would be built. Sometimes the putlog holes where scaffolding boards were fixed against the wall remain open and can be seen just above a tile course. The levels of tile courses are often different on the inner and outer facings of a wall. This is because the walls were so wide that there had to be a gang on each side. The gangs built their quotas of wall at different speeds and their stages of work might differ, so their tile courses do not match.

Tile course in wall.

An interesting point is that Roman cement was so tough that when modern engineers attempted to drill into the foundations of Richborough fort, their drills snapped. It was easier to break the stones than the Roman cement.

A characteristic of Roman building is the pink mortar, the colour being obtained by the inclusion of pounded brick. This is used on the outer face of the walls which shows more decoration than the inner face, having bonding courses of ironstone as well as tile and green sandstone.

On the surface

At first glance the present-day surface of the Roman fort appears to be just a grassy field but closer study will show that there are differences in level.

The excavated part of the north wall which has been left open, clearly shows the build-up of earthy material in that area since the fort was constructed. This is partly due to the natural accumulation which takes place on any area where there is vegetation, wind-blown dust and the debris of normal occupation. Archaeologists found a layer of black earth which had been deposited in this way during the Romano-British period, containing many remains from that time. However, above this in the eastern and southern parts of the fort is a thick layer of clay. This is believed to have come from the digging of the medieval moat and it accounts for the higher ground in those parts of the Roman fort.

There is also a ditch-like depression in the present-day surface, running north from the medieval castle to the Roman bastion which was added to by the Normans. It has been suggested that this may mark the original extent of the Norman bailey.

Excavation of the Roman surface has revealed many pits and much unevenness, suggesting that clay for tiles and building operations had been dug from inside the fort. In some places there were patches of mortar where it had been mixed by the workmen.

Anderita Roman Fort

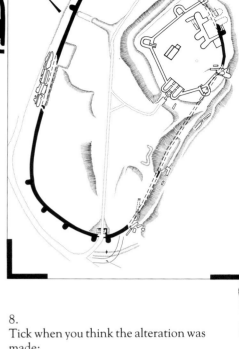

Pevensey Castle

You are going into the fort by the Roman West Gate. Before you enter, look to the left at the high walls and the bastions which have stood there for well over 1600 years. Roman guards patrolled the walls and their ballistas stood on top of the bastions ready for firing.

1.
You can see the remains of a wide ditch on the right of the present path into the fort. This once stretched across the entrance, joining the sea on the right with the harbour on the left. You may just be able to see the sea in the far distance over to the right.
Fill in the gaps in this sentence :
Pevensey was a peninsular. Digging the ditch made it into an

this made the fort   to defend.

2.
Walk through the Roman West Gate. Stop about fifty paces inside and turn so that the West Gate is on your left. Look at your plan of the fort. The parts marked in thick black were built by Romans and are still standing. Using your plan and looking around you - but not moving around - locate the following, ticking off each one as you find out where it is:

Roman West Gate ☐

Roman Postern in the north wall (on the left of the fallen part) ☐

Roman East Gate (this led to the harbour)

Medieval castle (built much later) in SE corner of the Roman fort ☐

Gap in the Roman wall to the south ☐

3.
Can you see the sea ?

In Roman times the sea was very close to this fort. Waves came nearly up to the southern wall and there were harbours on the eastern and northern sides of the fort. When there was a bad storm, spray from the sea splashed right over the southern wall, wetting the people inside.
Close your eyes for a moment and imagine yourself in Roman times in a storm. Shake off the spray. Open your eyes and look out to sea for any ships that may be in trouble. The slaves would be frantically rowing, trying to reach a sheltered harbour. Where will they make for ?

4.
Looking towards the south, what evidence can you see to tell you where the sea used to be ?

The ships of the Roman fleet were galleys, rowed by slaves. Stand in pairs in a line, or sit on the grass if it is dry. Pretend you are galley slaves, rowing as hard as you can to get to the harbour. Count the strokes : one, two, one, two .. when your teacher tells you to stop, walk over to the Roman East Gate to see where they would have landed.

5.
The Roman East Gate led to the harbour in those days. The fleet, that protected the coast from raiders and invaders and pirates, could safely anchor to take on supplies or repair damage to their ships. Merchant ships also came, with goods for sale to the soldiers and people who lived nearby.
The West Gate led overland.
Which gate is bigger and better fortified ?

6.
Why do you think the Romans built one gate bigger and stronger than the other ?

7. Stand inside the fort, facing the East Gate. Look at the bastion to your right. Can you see any evidence that this bastion has been altered? Write down what is different about it.

8.
Tick when you think the alteration was made:

In Roman times ☐

In the Middle Ages (medieval period) ☐

In Tudor times ☐

In the Second World War ☐

9.
Look around at other bastions and see if you can spot any other later alterations. Make a note of which bastion and how it has been altered.

10. Walk over to the North Postern where the Romans had a gateway. Amongst the pieces of fallen wall are some later additions to the fort. What do you think they are, and when were they made?

East Gate, Bastions and Walls.

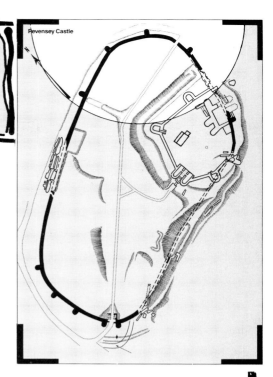
Pevensey Castle

Reminders : The East Gate led to the harbour in Roman times. Here, war galleys and merchant ships would unload supplies and soldiers for the fort. The galleys patrolled the sea to fight off or capture any pirates that might attack merchant ships, or raid the nearby villages.

1.
What do you think the Romans might do with any pirates they captured?

2.
Sketch the East Gate from inside the fort.

3.
Measure the width of the whole gate and the width and depth of the arch and enter these measurements on your sketch.

4.
Estimate the height of the whole gate and the height of the arch and enter these measurements on your sketch.

5.
Look at your plan of the site. Locate the four bastions nearest to the East Gate. There is one to the south (right side) of it, next to the medieval castle. The three others are to the left of the East Gate. Sharing the work between you and working from inside the fort, measure the distance between the towers and mark these measurements on your plan.

6.
Pace along the wall as if you were a sentry on guard duty between the bastions. If you have a watch, time how long it takes you and put the time on your plan.
How muck quicker can you cover the distance if you run? (In an emergency a sentry would have to be as quick as possible.)

7.
From inside the fort you can see that two of your four bastions have been altered, one in Norman times and one in the Second World War. Mark on your plan which one has the Norman addition and which was added to in the Second World War.

8.
Make a quick sketch of the alterations.

9.
When they were building the fort, separate groups of workers built the wall in sections. In some place, the wall is now falling apart in these sections. Make a note of how many sections you can see in your part of the wall up to the third bastion on the left of the East Gate.

10.
Working together, make up a play about an incident that might have happened in this part of the fort. Perhaps some captured pirates are brought in by the galleys, or someone very important comes to visit. About the time that this fort was built, the Roman Emperor visited Britain - he may even have come to inspect the fort. Act your play if you have time, or save it for when you get back to school.

11.
Working on your own, write down your impressions of this Roman fort of Anderita. Look around you and concentrate on what you see and what you feel about the place as it is now and as it was in the past.

The North Postern and the excavated wall section.

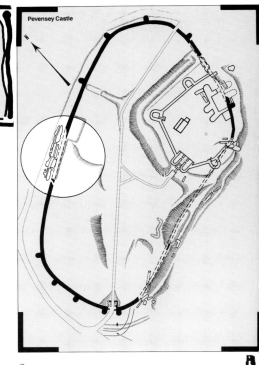

Pevensey Castle

1.
Find the notice which shows where the North Postern gate used to be. It doesn't look much like a gateway now, but if you look very carefully at the end of the upright piece of wall, you will see the beginning of a passage which went right through the wall. Make a sketch to show the pattern of the tiling in the wall where this entrance was.

2.
Does it looks as though the passage went straight through, or was it at an angle?

3.
The entrance to the passage from inside the fort was about 2.3m. How many soldiers do you think could stand in this entrance to fight off any intruders? (Remember they would need room to use their swords and daggers.)

4.
The outside entrance to the passage was probably only big enough to allow one person to enter at a time, and the passage was curved. What advantage would this have for the defenders of the fort if attackers tried to get in this way?

5.
Could an attacker have been fired upon from the wall walk or from a bastion?

6.
What do you think of an attacker's chances of getting into the fort through the North Postern?

7.
Move eastwards along the wall, to a rectangular depression where archaeologists have dug right down to the base of the Roman wall. For tasks 6, 7 and 8 you may have to go over the stile to the grassy area outside the wall.

DO NOT GO ON THE ROAD − IT IS VERY DANGEROUS.

How wide is the wall?

8.
Sharing the work, sketch the inside and the outside of the wall on a separate piece of paper. On your sketches make a note of the following:

(a) Places where the wall becomes narrower as it rises.

(b) The various kinds of building materials that have been used, e.g. stone, tile, flint, chalk, pebbles, etc.

(c) Your estimation of the height of the wall.

9.
From outside the fort, look up at the bastion. The Normans added something to it about 700 years after the Romans built it. What did the Normans add?

10.
From inside the fort, looking at the excavated wall section, suggest reasons why so much of the sandstone facing is missing. Who might have taken it, and what might they have done with it?

11.
Working together, make up a play about something which could have happened in this part of the fort. Perhaps a messenger comes through the postern, chased by attackers. Soldiers rush to defend the entrance. The man patrolling along top of the wall sees more attackers coming and sounds the alarm. Remember there was water on this side of the fort too, so the attackers would be in boats. Weapons are issued to the troops, the ballista is loaded. Finish the story or make up one of your own.
   If you have time, act your play. If not, save it for when you get back to school.

12.
Working on your own, write down your impressions of this Roman fort of Anderita. Look around you quietly, and concentrate on what you see and what you feel about the places. Think of it as it is now and as it was in the past.

Roman West Gate and Bastions

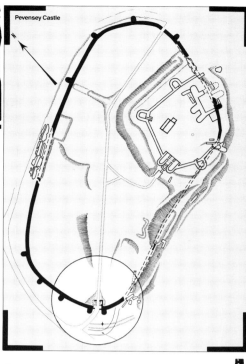

Pevensey Castle

Reminders : Anyone wishing to travel to or from the Roman fort overland had to go through the West Gate, for this was the only place where the peninsular joined the mainland. The West Gate was heavily fortified and an 5.4m. wide ditch was dug across this entrance, to make it difficult for attackers to get near the fort.

1.
What weapons might have been placed on the bastions to defend the fort?

2.
Write down your estimation of the height of the wall, near the tallest bastion:

(a) Height of wall inside the fort

(b) Height of wall outside the fort

3.
Why do you think there is a difference in the two heights?

4.
Look carefully at the bastions on each side of the gateway.
The Roman road ran between these. How far apart are they?

5.
About 700 years after the Romans left this fort, the Normans repaired it and built another gate between the bastions. What evidence of that gate can you find near the middle of the tallest bastion?

6.
Sketch one of the bastions. Label your sketch to show the different kinds of building materials that the Romans used.

7.
Add to your sketch, measurements of the width and depth of the bastion and an estimation of its height.

8.
Walk south from the gateway to the nearest point where the wall has collapsed. Go through to the other side, where you will find a Second World War addition to a fallen piece of Roman wall. What is it, and how can we tell it is not Roman?

9.
Working together, make up a play about something that could have happened at or near the West Gate in Roman times. You could include something about the changing of the guard, perhaps a messenger coming in to tell of an attack, or a spy trying to get into the fort in disguise. You can make up your own story as long as it takes place near the West Gate. If you have time, you can act the play here. If not, save it for when you get back to school.

10.
Working on your own, write down your impressions of this Roman fort of Anderita. Look around you quietly, and concentrate on what you see and what you feel about the place. Think of it as it is now and as it was in the past.

The whole frieze will tell the story of why and how Anderita was built, what it was like to live there, and the last battle. Each group will be asked to draw pictures for the frieze following a particular theme. Decide amongst yourselves what to draw. The number of pictures you produce will depend on the size of your group but you should try to cover all the most important aspects of your theme.

Here are some suggestions:

Pirates and raiders cause trouble, so the Romans plan to build a fort.

Possible subjects for pictures:
Saxon boats creep up a river to loot and burn a local village.
Roman surveyors mark out where the fort is to be.
Road builders make a road to the fort.

Building the fort
Getting the building materials and bringing them to the fort:
Woodcutters fell trees for timber.
Stonemasons quarry and shape stone.
Labourers dig for sand, mix mortar and pebbles.
Gangs of workmen dig foundations, and the outside ditch. Walls and gateways are built; tiles being laid at each stage.

Living in the fort
A banquet (special party with lots to eat) for an important visitor.
Soldiers arriving and training at the fort.
Soldiers departing.

The last days of the Britons in Anderita
Preparing for battle:
Spears, javelins, slings and darts being made ready.
Patrolling the wall-walk.
Reinforcements arrive secretly through the north postern.
The battle:
Defeat and death for the Britons.
Anderita is ruined and deserted.

Planning your picture.
Because your picture has to fit in with others, it is a good idea if everyone agrees to use the same size paper. Your work should be nicely coloured. You can check details of costume, weapons, etc. from books on Romans, Britons and Saxons.

Drama

You will be working in the same group as you were on your visit to Anderita. Remember the play you thought of during your visit? Now is the time to perform it really well.

Make sure of the story of your play.

Write down a list of characters. Give them Roman names. Go over the story together and make sure that everyone knows what is going to happen. One member of the group might like to write down what each person is going to say, although you need not stick to the exact words when actually performing your play.

Rehearsing. Find somewhere quiet where you can rehearse without being interrupted. Sort out where each person is to stand and any moving about that there should be. Make sure that you face the audience, particularly when you are speaking, or they may not hear you. Speak clearly and not too quickly. Go over the play several times until you all know your parts really well.

Noises off. These are background noises, such as the sound of horses hooves, the wind blowing, sounds of battle. Someone should be in charge of 'noises off' to make the noises at the appropriate times. You may like to play some suitable music at the beginning and end of your play.

Costume. Even if you cannot manage to make full costumes, it is a good idea to make enough to show who your characters are. For example, an important person could

wear a toga made out of a white sheet, soldiers could have helmets and swords made from cardboard.

Scenery. As with costume, you do not need to have anything elaborate. A gateway can be made out of two chairs, a bench can be a wall-walk. If the black or whiteboard is a suitable height, you could draw some background scenery on that. You may not be able to make scenery for your play, but you can design some. Draw a suitable background for one of the incidents in the play you thought of when you were at the fort. On a separate piece of paper, draw the people, animals, etc. that you would like to be in that scene. Colour them, cut them out and stick them onto your scenery.

Most important : really think yourself into the part.
Pretend that you were there!

Tape-recording your play.
You may like to record your play in this way, either instead of or as well as performing it. Just leaving a tape-recorder on during the performance does not usually give such a good result as making a special recording.

For this, it is more important to have a written script, so that there are no awkward pauses. Have your music and 'noises off' person ready.

Everyone should sit quietly round a table, with the tape-recorder and microphone in the middle.

Put plenty of expression into your voice. Speak clearly and not too quickly and try to sound as natural as you can.

© English Heritage 1991

Building materials

You may need to refer to notes about building materials, made on your visit to Anderita.

Fill in the missing letters of the following materials that were used to build the fort. Building materials

Gre . .   sandst . . .
Pl . . . .
. and
Cha . .
Ti . . .
. . mber
C . . y

Probable places of origin ☐

The forest of Andreadsweald ☐

The South Downs ☐

The sea-shore ☐

Stone quarry near Eastbourne ☐

Local tile kilns near the fort ☐

The South Downs Sand-pits at Pevensey ☐

Pits at the fort ☐

Making a scale drawing.
Use squared paper (1cm. squares if possible. Allow 1cm. (or 1 square) for each 1m. of real measurement. Re-draw the sketches you made at the fort onto your squared paper, with the correct measurements.

Enlarging your picture.
Draw a grid of larger squares on a larger piece of paper. Copy your picture, square by square, until it is finished. You can then trace the outline onto a clean sheet of paper without grid lines. Colour the picture if you wish.

Symmetry.
A plane figure that is symmetrical can be folded in half exactly. The line of the fold is called the axis of symmetry.

The groundplan of the Roman bastions at Anderita consists of a square joined to a semi-circle. Draw the groundplan of a bastion using a 4cm. square and a semi-circle with a radius of 2cm.

Find the axis of symmetry and draw it on your plan. Explain how you found the axis.

Modelling the fort.
Because the fort is so large it may not be possible to model all of it. So each group will model the part of the fort which it particularly studied. To make a scale model you will need the drawings you have already made. Don't forget to make thick walls. You will need:

Piece of flat wood, hardboard or firm cardboard for the base. Crumpled newspaper for the rubble insides of the walls.

Thin cardboard for the stone outsides of the walls.

Scissors and sellotape.
Paints, felt pens, crayons or coloured pencils.

Method:
Use the measurements you took on your visit to make a plan on your baseboard of the part of the castle that you intend to model.

Use your scale drawing to cut out the right size and shapes for the outside and inside walls.

Attach crumpled paper to base to form inside of walls. Attach card to base for outside walls. Colour outside walls, not forgetting lines of tiles. (Remember the colours you saw during your visit.)

To add a wall-walk to your model, turn over the top portion of the inside wall and attach this with sellotape to the outside wall, thus covering the crumpled inside filling. It will turn over more easily if you fold it before attaching it to your model.

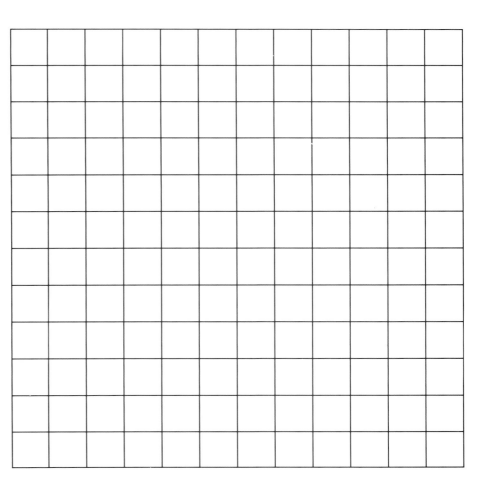

VII

Defence and Attack

After the visit
Activities

1.
Defenders
You are the Commander of Anderita. Look at your plan of the fort. You will notice that most of the bastions are at the curved ends of the fort. This is so that defenders can be placed to fire on attackers, often from two directions.

Owing to the many Saxon raids, you have only 10 men left who are experts with the sling-shot and another attack is coming. Pretend that the fort is not ruined. Where would you place your men to give them the best chance of driving away the attackers? Give reasons for your answer.

2.
Attackers
This time you are the leader of a large attacking force. Again, supposing the fort to be in good condition, where would you think was the best place to attack it?

If an open attack did not work, how else might you defeat the defenders?

3.
Your teacher will read you two accounts of what really happened to the defenders in the last battle between the Saxon invaders and the Romano-British occupants of the fort. Both accounts were written some time after the event. We do not know how accurate they are but archaeologists found spear and javelin heads and small pieces of iron pointed at both ends, possibly the heads of darts. These were lying at the top of the black earth of the Roman layer.

Write a poem about the last battle. Decorate it with small drawings if you wish.

4.
The Saxons who had killed all the Romano-British people in Anderita, combined with other invaders to take over much of Britain. The Roman ways died out. The new people did not know how to build in stone. Even their grandest buildings were made of wood.

Some years afterwards, an Anglo-Saxon poet wrote about the condition of the old Roman buildings. The language he uses is old-fashioned and there may be some words that you do not know. Here is a list to help you:
wondrous = wonderful
pinnacles = spires or the pointed tops of towers
tumult = noisy activity
pestilence = fatal illness affecting many people
multitude = a very large number of people

Read the passage carefully, referring to the above list for words those meanings you do not know.

"Wondrous is this wall-stone; broken by fate, the castles have decayed; the work of giants is crumbling. Roofs are fallen, ruinous are the towers.... frost is on their cement, broken are the roofs,.....undermined by age....

Bright were the castle-dwellings, many the bath-houses, lofty the host of pinnacles, great the tumult of men.... till Fate the mighty overturned that. The wide walls fell; days of pestilence came; death swept away all the bravery of men; their fortresses became waste places; the city fell to ruin. The multitudes who might have built it anew lay dead on the earth."

(a) Write down any words or phrases that show the Anglo-Saxon writer was impressed with the old buildings.

(b) What does he say has caused the decay?

(c) He mentions 'Fate the mighty' but does not mention any invaders or battles. Why do you think this is?

(d) Who were 'the multitudes who might have built it anew?' Why could they not rebuild their 'castle-dwellings.'

(e) Do you think the writer regrets what has happened?
Give a reason for your answer.

VII

© English Heritage 1991

Medieval Castle
— History

No written records have survived to tell us whether the early Saxons made use of the Roman fort they had captured. Gradually, even the name Anderita disappeared from the language. However, we do know that the harbour continued to be used. The Anglo-Saxon Chronicle has several entries which tell of ships putting into the port of Pevensey which grew up there and from which the medieval castle took its name. Earl Godwin and his sons landed there a number of times during the reign of Edward the Confessor, the last Saxon king.

The Normans at Pevensey

The Roman fort was an added bonus and the Normans quickly adapted it to their needs. The eastern end was cut off with palisade and ditch and a wooden tower, soon to be replaced by one of stone, was built in the south-eastern corner. Essential repairs to gates, walls and towers were carried out and a Roman tower at the north-west corner of the new inner bailey was heightened, perhaps to provide an observation point, for in the early days they might still have feared a counter-attack from the north.

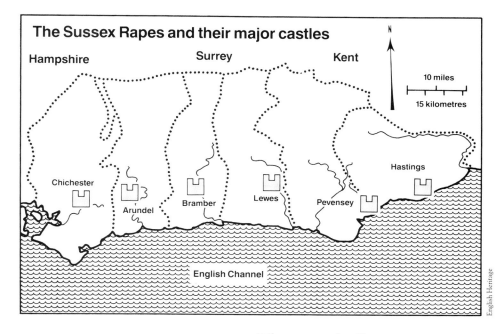

The Sussex Rapes and their major castles

Hampshire Surrey Kent

N

10 miles
15 kilometres

Chichester
Arundel
Bramber
Lewes
Pevensey
Hastings

English Channel

English Heritage

Soon, even that fear passed. Harold and his brothers, who might have led the English, had all been killed in the battle. Sussex was divided into five areas called Rapes. William gave each Rape to a close friend or relative.

Thirteenth Century repairs

The pigeon house was cleaned, plastered and thatched and new perches and openings were made. The bridge and drawbridge were renewed and the windows in the keep were mended. From AD 1275 to AD 1277 there were repairs to the chapel, the hall, the stable and the Queen's chamber, roofs were repaired and an upper chamber (solar) built in the North Tower.

BELOW: Reconstruction drawing showing Pevensey Castle during the first phase of Norman occupation in about AD 1066. Notice the inner bailey wall is a wooden palisade defence.

English Heritage Photo Library

The armaments of the castle also received attention. Mangonels and crossbows were overhauled. Two large keys were made, probably for winding up the mangonels and 9d. was spent on hemp for cords. The armour in the castle was polished; lard, bran and a leather sack being bought for that purpose. At this time, the armour kept there consisted of 7 hauberks, 1 corslet, 3 pairs of greaves, 2 head-pieces and 1 crupper.

The moat was either cleaned or altered. In AD 1280, six men were employed for a week to break through the end of it and let out the water. The fish from the moat were taken to a pond called 'la Crumble', presumably to be stored there for restocking the moat when the work had been completed.

In AD 1280, extensive works began at Pevensey which were to last three years. Apart from general refurbishing of the buildings, the focus of this work was on the main gate, the first year on the south and the second year on the north part. The account of William Cropp, foreman of the works of the castle, gives us fascinating glimpses of these activities.

Master Simon seems to have been the senior mason in charge of shaping and laying the stones; he earned 2s.0d (10p) a week. William Masson was the next most highly paid at 21d. (about 9p). Roger de Ore and two other masons were each paid 18d. (7½p) a week. As well as local stone, 95 blocks were brought to Pevensey by sea from Caen. The five masons were assisted by nine other men. Two spent their time digging stones and cement from 'under the wall of the castle which was thrown down in the war.' This material was presumably reused either in the foundations or as rubble filling. Two men operated windlasses over the gate to raise stones and mortar. One man received these on the scaffolding and helped to lay the stones on the tower. For most of them, the work went on that year for 14 weeks and 3 days. The carriers of stones were paid 9d. (4p) a week for eight weeks, but 10d (4½p) for the eight and a half weeks of harvest time.

Payments were also made for supporting activities. Twelve carts brought 'beams of beech' to make the scaffolding. 300 large withies, 100 small withies, large and small nails were also needed. Picks, axes, chisels, adzes and other tools had to be pointed and sharpened many times. Four mortars, a sieve, a handcart and a hurdle were bought for the men who were making mortar. A cooper was employed for ten days to hoop buckets, barrels and buts. Fifty sheaves of furze were bought to put under the winch, as well as cords for lifting up 'stones, mortar and other things'.

As well as the work on the gate, timber was brought in to make stairs and a new bridge in front of the door of the keep. Two sawyers sawed posts, beams, planks, etc. for 13½ days for 9s.0d. (45p). Two carpenters made the bridge, scaffolding, windlasses,

winch and 'other things needed in the castle.' They were paid a high wage for those times (15p) a week each and presumably had to pay their assistants out of it. Another carpenter received 15d (6p) a week. 2000 bolting and 150 large nails were bought for the work. The accounts do not say where these came from but it is probable that they were produced by ironworkers in the Weald.

It seems that most of the work on the southern part of the gate was finished by the end of September AD 1280. The main workforce departed, leaving just a few men to finish off and tidy up. In AD 1281, Master Simon was paid £17.17s.8d. 'for building the north part of the gate.' Presumably he organised and paid his own masons that year. He was, however, supplied with the necessary building materials. Payments are recorded for 360 horseloads of lime, burnt at Willingdon using a large quantity of sea coal (bought at Seaford and elsewhere) and firewood from 'Clavrigg.' 2100 stones were bought at the quarry, 500 of which were brought in by sea during the winter (when presumably the roads were impassable) and the other 1600 brought direct to the castle in the summer. Forty two more blocks of Caen stone also arrived by sea, as well as thirty seven boat loads of sand. Men were again employed to dig for stone 'around the castle, in the town of Pevensey and elsewhere.'

The later history of Pevensey

By Tudor times, however, the sea had receded from Pevensey, which greatly lessened the castle's defensive value. The once-extensive sheltered harbour silted up and became farmland and marsh. The port was no longer needed as an embarkation point for Normandy. Even though the existence of an artillery chamber in the keep in AD 1420 suggests that the castle may have been armed, weapons in those days had not enough range to make Pevensey Castle a good coastal defence point once the sea had receded. It ceased to be inhabited, fell into decay and was plundered by the neighbourhood. An inventory of AD 1543 reported that it was

The demi-culverin.

not worth repairing and that the stone and leadwork were being stolen. Some of the stone was sold to John Thacker, or Thatcher, one of the local gentry, who built a fine house called Priesthawes not far away.

However, although the castle was not a lot of use for defence, it could still have provided a secure foothold for an invader. For this reason, when the country was threatened by the Spanish Armada, the castle was recommended either to be put in order or completely taken down. It does not seem as though either of these recommendations was followed but it was armed with two demi-culverins. One of these is now in the Tower of London and the other can be seen in the inner bailey at Pevensey Castle. It is a cast-iron gun, manufactured in the Weald and marked with a Tudor Rose and the initial ER (Elizabeth Regina). In the outer bailey is a small gun emplacement which is believed to have been constructed at that time (AD 1587-88).

After the defeat of the Armada, the castle seems to have been left to decay, although estimates were made of the value of its materials. Because of the strength of its walls attempts to demolish it were largely unsuccessful. There were several private owners, the last of whom presented it as a gift to the State in October 1925.

BELOW : Pevensey Castle seen from opposite the Roman east gate. An engraving by Samuel and Nathaniel Buck, 1737.

Description

The Curtain Walls surround the inner bailey, the outer bailey being formed by the Roman walls. They have three round-fronted towers and date from the mid-thirteenth century. They were originally crenellated but the battlements have now gone. Walls and towers are ashlar faced.

The Towers in the Curtain Wall originally had similar internal arrangements. There was a basement reached by a flight of steps from the courtyard, with a branch staircase leading from these steps to a postern door. This opened onto a wide ledge (the berm) by the moat. The ground floor rooms were approached from the court yard through a lobby, as was the garderobe.

The first floor was apparently reached only from the wallwalks, the line of which can be seen at several points from the inner bailey. There were fireplaces in the upper rooms. The basement of the NW tower is better finished than the others with a stone vault on sculptured corbels.

The interiors of the towers were adapted in 1940 as quarters for the troops who garrisoned the castle, with inner skins of brickwork, wooden floors, glazed windows and new roofs. Most of these are still in place in the S and NE towers. Stone balls, believed to have been stored and possibly manufactured at Pevensey for medieval throwing weapons, can be seen in these two towers.

The Gatehouse was originally built before the curtain walls but was extensively rebuilt in AD 1280-1282. It incorporates a number of defensive features, remains of which can still be seen. There is a drawbridge pit beneath the present wooden bridge in front of the entrance and the remains of portcullis grooves can be seen ending near to ground level on the south side and at a higher level on the north side. A 'murder hole' is built into the roof of the gateway passage. This barbican gateway has two towers. Each has a basement with fine ashlar walls. The basement of the S tower is approached by a staircase and slots in the wall by the door show that it could be barred from the outside. The basement of the north tower is reached by a trapdoor and presumably was intended as an oubliette. The original doorway into the north tower could also be barred from the outside. It seems likely, therefore, that both of the barbican towers were used as prisons. Remains of a fireplace can be seen in the north tower.

The Well was opened in the nineteenth century by Mr. Gun, constable, port-reeve, overseer, market-clerk and custodian of the castle. It was found to have a diameter of 2.2m lined with ashlar. Its walls are vertical for 12m gradually contracting until a depth of 15m is reached and narrowing to a 60cm square framework of solid oak. Catapult balls of various diameters and 'skulls of wolves' were found in the well. The well was originally contained in a well house but no traces of this remain.

The Chapel foundations can be seen in the courtyard and their form suggests a Norman date. When it was excavated in 1852 three graves were found below the chancel floor, containing six skeletons, three of them children. On the right and left of the chancel steps were two small stone enclosures, possibly to support a pulpit and reading desk. Opposite the S door and 3.5m from the W end was the font in situ. The roof of the chapel, consisting of thick slates marked with broad red veins, had fallen in upon the font. It was judged that the chapel had been destroyed by fire. Many iron arrow-heads 10 to 15cm in length were found amongst the debris. Later medieval records mention a chapel in the keep. An account of AD 1281 mentions repairs to the thatched roof of the chapel. No doubt many changes were made during the long history of the castle buildings.

The Keep was built into the eastern Roman wall of the castle. A large part of this wall has now collapsed, together with the east wall of the keep but the shell of most of the other three sides of the keep remains visible. Its internal measurements are 16.8 × 9m. There were no openings in the ground floor, the keep being entered via a covered stairway and bridge through an iron door at first floor level. The finish of the masonry suggests that the ground floor was hollow and originally formed a dungeon. The site of the entrance is unknown but may have been between the two apsidal projections on the west face.

Apart from its defensive uses, the keep contained the Constable's living quarters, a kitchen and a chapel. The rooms had glazed windows. There seems to have been a constant need for repairs to the lead roof and the wooden joists which supported it. A granary tower adjoined the keep.

Other buildings. The presence of other buildings in the inner bailey is indicated by the remains of chimneys which can be seen on the inside of the curtain walls. Accounts for repairs and reports on the condition of the castle at various times in the medieval period survive. From these we know that there was a Hall with bedrooms adjoining. Another suite of rooms comprised the Queen's room next to the chapel and other rooms adjoining. The chapel had a paling fence around it. There was a stable and a pigeon house. These domestic buildings were timber-framed, infilled with lath and plaster and pugged with earth on the outside. They were whitewashed and mostly thatched, although the hall is mentioned as having 6000 tiles laid upon it and a carpenter was paid to make shingles (wooden tiles). Inside, the principal rooms were panelled.

BELOW : The medieval castle from the south.

English Heritage

Second World War

In 1940 the Germans occupied France and threatened to invade England. With the coming of modern weapons, Pevensey Castle again had a part to play in the country's defence. It was refortified for use as an observation and command post in May 1940 but modern weapons required a different strategy. In Roman and medieval times, the need had been for a conspicuously strong castle that would deter potential attackers. To fulfil its modern role, and be safe from air attack, the castle had to look ruinous and abandoned.

Pillbox by North Postern.

Pillboxes for machine guns and observation points were cunningly built amongst the Roman and medieval ruins. A particularly good example can be seen in the fallen south wall near the Roman West Gate, where lines of red brick were incorporated into modern concrete in imitation of Roman concrete, to look as much as possible like the ruined Roman wall nearby. Elsewhere, pillboxes were built into bastions and towers and other fallen Roman walls, as well as at the foot of the east side of the medieval keep. The keep itself was beyond repair but the towers of the medieval castle were fitted up as living accommodation. The Roman West Gate was closed by a blockhouse for anti-tank defence.

From May 1940 until 1944, the castle was continuously occupied by regular troops and by the Home Guard. Early in 1944, the US Army Corps used it as a direction centre.

After the war, the castle was taken back into the care of the State. Most of the twentieth century additions were left as evidence of this latest important phase of its existence; the only major building that was removed was the blockhouse.

ABOVE RIGHT: Pillbox built into the remains of fallen Roman masonry.
RIGHT: Pillboxes hidden in the keep and curtain walls commanding the flat land to the south of the castle.

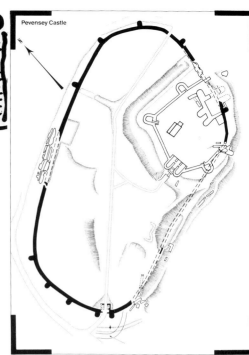

Pevensey Castle

The Normans invaded England in 1066. There were not many of them compared to the Saxons who lived here. They needed a safe place for themselves and their animals. They took over the old Roman fort at Pevensey. New gates were needed as well as other repairs

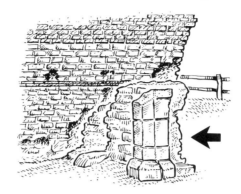

1.
You can still see a small part of the Norman gate attached to a Roman tower (bastion) at the West Gate. How wide was the Norman gate? (Assume there would have been a similar wall attached to the right-hand bastion.)

2.
The old Roman ditch outside the West Gate had silted up so the Normans dug another one. What must they have put over the ditch so that they could enter the castle through the West Gate?

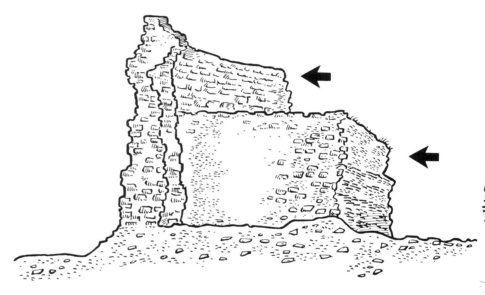

3.
Go through the Roman West Gate. Around you are the Roman walls. The sea was very close to the castle, nearly up to the walls on the south side.

Walk over to the medieval castle. When you reach the moat, turn left towards the highest tower in the Roman wall. Find a ditch. Notice that it follows in the same direction as part of the moat. Label that part of the moat and the ditch Norman on your plan. Label the other part of the moat Medieval.

4.
When the Normans came, there was no stone castle. They cut off part of the Roman fort with a palisade (fence) and the Norman ditch you have labelled on your plan. Where the stone castle now is, they built a tall wooden tower. This eastern area of the Roman fort became the inner bailey of the Norman castle. Write Norman Bailey on your plan (between the East Gate and the high tower in the Roman wall.)

5.
Follow the ditch along to the high tower. Complete this sketch of the upper part of the tower. Label the upright piece of wall Norman. The little square building on top of the tower is later. Label it on your sketch Second World War.

There are square holes in the Norman wall. These are called beam-slots. What were they for? How many are there?

6.
Suggest a reason why the Normans made this tower higher. (Clue : they feared a Saxon attack.)

7.
Walk over to the East Gate. The Normans rebuilt this. If you are allowed to go outside the East Gate, stand on the pavement by the seats. Look to your left (north) and you will see the pattern of the Norman repairs on the Roman tower there.

DO NOT GO ON THE ROAD — IT IS VERY DANGEROUS.

On your plan, next to this tower, write Norman Repairs.

Defences from outside

Pevensey Castle

From outside the medieval castle, you can see that part of the Norman moat was filled in and a new section was dug, running east-west to join up with the remaining part. Inside this, instead of the earlier palisade, they built the stone curtain wall and towers. A fortified (barbican) gateway was made, guarded by its own two towers.

Starting inside the Roman East Gate, inspect as much of the outside of the medieval castle as you can without going outside the castle grounds. Answer the following questions as you walk around:

1. The Moat

How wide is the moat? (Measure across the bridge.)

Does it go all round the castle Yes/No

If not, why do you think this is?

Which part of the moat is full of water and which part is dry?

Do you think a dry moat can be a good defence of a castle in medieval times?

Write down anything else you have noticed that is interesting about the moat.

2. The Curtain Wall and its three towers

Estimate the height of one of the towers.

Are the towers higher than the curtain wall? Yes/No

If they are, why do you think this is?

What shape are the towers? Round/Square

Are they the same size all the way up?

If not, why is this?

How many medieval towers are there in the curtain wall?
(Do not include the towers which belong to the gateway.)

Count and write down the number of arrow slits in one tower.

Write down any other interesting features that you notice in the curtain wall and its towers.

3. The Gateway

There was once a drawbridge over the moat. The pit which the bridge swung into when it was being raised is still there. Look under the present bridge, near the entrance. Don't fall in!

How wide is the pit? (Measure along the bridge.)

How deep is it? (Estimate)

In what way or ways are the towers of the barbican gate differently built from those in the curtain wall? (Clue: shape.)

At the entrance to the gate, find the partly ruined grooves where the portcullis used to raised and lowered.

How can you tell that the grooves stopped just above ground level?

Why was that?

Look up into the roof of the barbican gate for the murder hole. How was it used?

Make a note of any other interesting things that you notice about the barbican gate.

Defences from inside

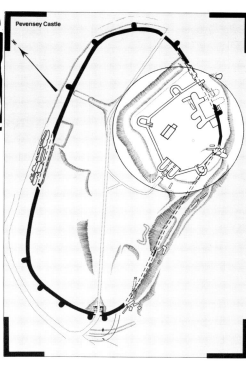

Pevensey Castle

Your teacher will probably divide you into groups for some of the tasks on this sheet. When you have finished your own work, look at the other parts of the castle and make a note of anything interesting or puzzling that you see.

1.
The Towers in the Curtain Wall (NOT the gateway) were all built to a similar plan but each is now different inside. Try to visit them all and answer the questions for at least one of them. Put your answers in the boxes provided.

	NE TOWER	NW TOWER	S TOWER
Stone store?			
Stairs. How many?			
Arrow slits. How many visible from inside/outside!			
Stone carving.			
Room below ground. Suggest use.			
Door to moatside. Suggest use.			
20th century alterations. Suggest reason.			

In the Inner Bailey :
2.
Measure the height of one tower using the ruler method.

3.
Measure the height of one section of the standing wall using the ruler method.

4.
What evidence can you see that there was once a walkway around the top of the wall?

5.
Make a quick sketch of the Postern Gate with estimated measurements of its width and height.

6.
How near to the Postern Gate do you think the sea was in early medieval times? Suggest a possible use for the Postern Gate.

7.
Go round to the back (east side) of the keep, where you can view the remains of the inside. Measure and write down
(a) its width
(b) its length
(c) its height (estimate).

8.
Make a note of any evidence you can see that there was more than one floor to the keep - you could make a quick sketch to show what you mean.

9.
How thick were the walls of the keep?

Living in the castle

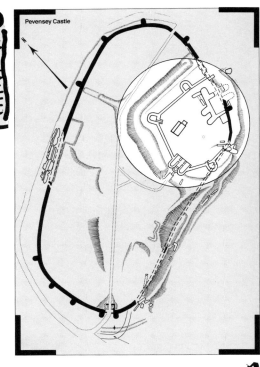

Pevensey Castle

1.
At first, the only living quarters were in the keep because that was the safest place. Later, when the wooden palisade was replaced by strong stone walls, a 'great hall', where the people could live and eat, was built against one wall. Bedrooms were attached to the hall.

Look carefully at the walls of the inner bailey to find the remains of fireplaces and chimneys. Mark their positions on your plan.

2.
Religion was very important to people in medieval times. Find the foundations of the chapel.

How many people do you think the chapel could have held at one time?

> Either draw the font, showing details of the carving, or draw the gravestone, showing the pattern on it.

3.
For many years, Pevensey Castle belonged to the Queens of England. The Queen's rooms were next to the Chapel. Why do you think there are no remains of these buildings? Give two possible reasons.

4.
The kitchen would probably also have been built against the wall, but well away from other buildings because of the danger of fire.
Which fireplace is well away from the others and so might have belonged to the kitchen? Mark it on your plan.

5.
As well as all these buildings, there were stables for the horses and a dovecote. The keep was still used and could be lived in if necessary. Food, arms and ammunition could be safely stored there. Mark on your plan where you think the stables were.

6.
In the event of an attack, it was most important for the defenders to have plenty of food and water inside the castle. In those days, the well was in a well house. Find the well and mark it on your plan.

7.
The Gatehouse towers were nearly as strong as the keep. Walk towards the Gatehouse. The north tower is on the right of the gate as you look out from the castle. To get inside, we now go through a space where the east wall of the tower is missing. Just inside, is the original doorway into this tower. Slots at each side of the door held a bar which stopped the door from being opened from the inside. What does this tell you about the use of this room?
Tick which you think is right:

The room was a guardhouse. ☐
The room was a prison. ☐

8.
An oubliette was a place, usually below ground level, where prisoners were put to be forgotten and die. There was no need for a door. Find the oubliette in this Gatehouse tower and mark it on your plan.

9.
Explore the other Gatehouse tower. Write down a particular feature that makes you think this tower may have been used as a prison.

Make a note of anything else that is different from the other tower, or that particularly interests you.

> **10.**
> Either join with your group in making up a play about living in the castle in medieval times or find a quiet corner by yourself and make up a poem about life in the castle.

Norman additions to the Roman fort

After the visit Activities

1.
When the Normans invaded Saxon England, they needed a base, so they took over and altered the old Roman fort at Pevensey. Using your plan as a guide, draw a plan of the fort and castle that the Normans built. Activity Sheet No.1 which you completed at the castle will help you. Remember that the medieval stone castle was not there in Norman times but they would have built a wooden tower about where the keep is now. Remember that the Norman ditch was different from the present moat.

2.
Underneath your plan, make a list of all the alterations and repairs that the Normans had to make to the Roman fort.

3.
Why did the Normans make the Roman fort smaller?

4.
Find some pictures of Normans and their boats. Using these as a guide make up your own picture or collage of the Norman landing. (A good guide would be the Bayeux Tapestry.)

5.
Find out more about the Norman Conquest. Why did William think he had the right to be King of England? How did he treat the Saxon people?

6.
Write an imaginary conversation either between two Saxons, or between two Normans soon after Norman invasion. They are discussing what will happen next.

Defences from outside

After the visit Activities

1.
Using the information which you collected at the castle, write a full description, with measurements, of that part of the outside of the castle which you inspected. Illustrate your report with a picture or a plan.

2.
The crenellations (or battlements) that used to be along the top of the curtain wall and the towers are now ruined and missing. Why were these important to the defence of a castle?

3.
Why were round towers considered to be stronger for defence than square ones? (Clue: think about undermining.)

4.
Make a project book, drawings, paintings or collage showing the different types of defences at Pevensey. Use your own notes and diagrams plus any pictures you can find of parts of the defences that were missing, e.g. a portcullis. Draw or collect pictures of weapons that were in use in medieval times.

5.
Write a conversation between two soldiers as they arrive with Simon de Montfort's forces to besiege the castle.

6.
Imagine that there are three attackers (X, Y and Z) who are trying to climb the ladders they have put against the castle wall. The constable of the castle can only spare two archers to defend this part of the castle. Where should he place them so that they have the best chance of preventing the attackers from reaching the top of the wall? Give reasons for your answer.

7.
Would it be better for the archers to be on top of the towers firing through the battlements, or in the towers firing through the arrow slits? Give reasons for your answer.

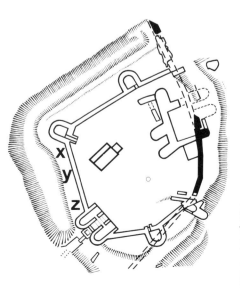

1.
Discuss the following questions with other members of your group, then write and illustrate a full account of the tower which you particularly studied.
(a) Why do you think there was so much stone shot?
(b) What kinds of weapons would have fired this shot?
(c) What sort of local stone might have been used to make this shot?
(d) Were you able to get into every part of 'your' tower or were there other floors above or below which it is no longer possible to reach? If so, why?
(e) What evidence was there of other floors or rooms in your tower?

2.
Choose one of your group to present an account of 'your' tower to the class. Discuss the differences between the towers and the purpose of each tower.
Write down:
Which two towers were most alike? Which seems to be the 'odd one out'. Give careful reasons for your answer.

3.
Using the measurements of a tower and a section of the curtain wall which you wrote down at the castle, make a scale drawing using the scale 2cm = 1m to show the height of the tower and curtain wall.

4.
Measure the length of the curtain wall on your plan of the medieval castle and turn this into metres using the scale on the plan.
Do the same for the Roman wall.
How much longer was the Roman curtain wall?

5.
What main advantage was there for the Normans and medieval people in making their castle smaller than the Roman fort?
(Clues : defence, number of defenders)
What main disadvantage might there have been in having a smaller castle?

6.
Using books in your classroom and/or the library, find out how the various rooms in a medieval keep were furnished and used. Show this information in a drawing or diagram.
    Which parts of the keep were most important for the defence of the castle?
    Why were the walls of the keep made so thick?

7.
In what ways did weapons and ammunition change between medieval and Tudor times?

8.
Imagine Pevensey Castle was being attacked. The defenders have:
1. Good archers.
2. Two mangonels and plenty of ammunition as well as soldiers to fire them.
3. Good swordsmen.
4. Enough food and water for four months.

Attackers have:
1. Good archers.
2. A siege tower.
3. Ladders.
4. Two mangonels and some ammunition.
5. A battering ram.
6. Miners with gunpowder.
7. Good swordsmen.

Answer these questions in words or with a diagram. (Assume that each side has 20 archers, 15 swordsmen and gunners to fire the mangonels.)
(a) Where should the defenders place their archers?
(b) Where should the defenders place their swordsmen?
(c) Where should the attackers concentrate their attack?
(d) What should the attackers be attempting to achieve with each of their weapons?

(e) If the attackers cannot succeed in taking the castle by assault, in what other way or ways could they force them to surrender?

The following extract about a siege of Rochester Castle may help you to answer. Roger of Wendover described the attack by King John in 1215.

    … as well as the stones hurled from the catapults and slings and the missiles of the crossbow men and archers, frequent attacks were made by the knights and their followers. When some were tired, other fresh ones took their place in the attack, which allowed the besieged no rest… The siege lasted many days owing to the great bravery and boldness of the besieged who hurled stone for stone and weapon for weapon… on the enemy.
    …The food of the besieged also began to fail and they had to eat horses and even their costly chargers. The king also used miners to undermine the walls, first the outer wall of the castle and then the keep. At last, not a scrap of food remaining…all the garrison left the castle and surrendered to the king. They were nearly all unhurt, except for one knight who had been killed by an arrow…

1.

The Great Hall which was built against the wall of the inner bailey was not made of stone. We know this because it sometimes had to be repaired. Some of the accounts for the repairs have survived. In 1302 the hall was fitted with gutters made of timber and lined with lead. It was partly thatched and partly tiled. Some of the woodwork was renewed and the walls were plastered and whitewashed. Most of the materials for these repairs came from places in the Rape of Pevensey.

Here are some examples:

Timber beams for the hall and rooms next to it were cut and squared in 'Mersefeud park.'

Timber for the ridge rafters came from 'Coudenn.'

6 acres of rushes were cut, spread out to dry and collected in 17 carts from 'Wylendon.'

Earth to plaster the Hall was brought from the 'Hospital' to the castle in 45 barrows.

38 rafters came from 'Chidingelegh.'

Lathes (thin strips of wood) and props were brought from the 'Forest of Essesdoun.'

400 boards of beech for panelling came from 'Assesdon.'

(a) What does the above information tell you about the state of goods transport in those days?

(b) 'Essesdoun' and 'Assesdon' are different spellings of the same place. Why should they have been spelt differently? Discuss this with your teacher.

Why has it been necessary to standardise the spelling of place-names in modern times?

(c) What does the contribution of 'Wylendon' tell you about the place in those days?

2.

With others in your group, draw pictures to make a frieze telling the story of the repairs to the Great Hall. Include the trees being cut down in Maresfield Park, rushes being cut and brought from Willingdon etc. Finish with a picture of the Great Hall itself.

Map:

Pevensey Rape

Ashdown Forest

5 miles

5 kilometres

Part of Hastings Rape

Maresfield

Battle

Ashburnham

Chiddingley

Herstmonceux

Hailsham

Wertling

Old coastline

Claverham

Lewes

Couden

Westham

Pevensey

Crumble pond

The South

Downs

Willingdon

The beach

Seaford

Eastbourne

British Sea (English Channel)

3.

Find out about medieval kitchens, their methods of cooking and the food they ate. Describe a meal prepared for the King and Queen when they visited Pevensey Castle.

4.

In 1360, there was danger of invasion from France. The castle was garrisoned with a small force of trained men-at-arms, archers, and a watchman. If necessary, they would have been assisted by other local men. The following food was provided for the defenders: Sacks of wheat and beans, wine, salt, chick-peas, 3 oxen, 20 muttons, 10 pigs for bacon. How does this food compare with the meal for the King and Queen that you described. What else would have been needed to keep the garrison healthy?

5.

Some important prisoners were kept at Pevensey. One of these was Queen Joan, stepmother of Henry IV, who accused her of witchcraft, and took away her lands. She had to pay for her support at Pevensey castle but was apparently treated kindly by Sir John Pelham the constable of the castle who sent nine servants to look after her on her way there.

Eventually the king, who had really only wanted her fortune, let her go and gave her back her property.

Look at the notes and information about the various buildings which you collected during your visit to the castle. Decide which building you think Queen Joan lived in whilst she was there (remember she was treated well.) Either write a story or make up a poem or draw a series of pictures with captions, based on the story of Queen Joan's arrest and imprisonment in Pevensey Castle.

QUIZ

Who put it there?

Where is it?

What is it?

Where is it?

What is it?

Why was it important?

Where is it?

What is it?

QUIZ

QUIZ

Where is it?

What is it?

Where is it?

What is it?

Wordsearch

F	S	Y	E	L	L	A	G	P	A
K	L	T	T	A	O	M	E	I	N
L	D	I	T	C	H	I	P	R	D
A	R	L	N	E	L	T	S	A	C
W	S	E	A	T	H	T	H	T	S
B	A	S	T	I	O	N	I	E	N
L	O	P	O	D	R	O	W	S	O
L	V	E	W	W	E	L	L	F	X
A	E	A	E	P	T	R	D	O	A
W	A	R	R	O	W	S	T	E	S

Find the following words:

BASTION	CASTLE	PIRATES	TOWER
FLINT	GALLEYS	TILES	WELL
DITCH	SEA	WALL WALK	ARROWS
SPEAR	SWORD	SAXONS	MOAT

Arrange your words under these headings:
Defences
Building material
Weapons
Attackers
Which words do not fit in?
What heading(s) would you put the odd words under?

Riddle
My first is in tick
but not in tock
My second's in sheep
but not in shock
My third is the vowel
Used most of all
My fourth is in peep
And also in pop
My whole was wide
And also tall
And meant to be
A safe place for all.

Draw me!

Teachers' notes for activities.

Teachers may photocopy the plan of Pevensey on page 4 for any of the activities in this book.

Anderita

Activity 1

1.
Digging the ditch across the western (landward) end of the peninsular made it into an island, which would have been easier to defend.

2.
If the children stand with the Roman West Gate on their left, the North Postern will be in the wall facing them, the East Gate and medieval castle on their right and the fallen south wall behind them.

3.
The galleys may have come into a harbour on the south west (a short way outside the West Gate, but since most gales are south-westerly, they would find better shelter on the north side of the fort. There is still some doubt as to the exact locations of the harbour(s) during Roman times.

4.
The land falls sharply away from the fort and is fairly flat to the present coastline. Most of this area was under water.

5.
The West Gate is much larger and better fortified.

6.
This is a question to invite speculation. Suggestions might be that any attack coming from the landward side might be very serious (not just a raid) and therefore good defences would be needed at that point. Important visitors would probably have arrived from that direction so the most impressive gate was built there. the East Gate could have been more of a 'back door' where goods or soldiers coming by sea could enter the fort.

7 and 8.
There is a notice giving the date (1939-1945) of the modern pill-box which has been added to the bastion.

9.
Small children will not be tall enough to see most of the bastions from the inside but the third one on the left of the East Gate has a Norman addition which makes it easily visible. It was probably heightened to make a look-out tower soon after the Norman invasion of 1066, associated with a wooden motte and bailey castle which preceded the medieval castle. There is a modern addition within the ruins of the Norman alteration.

10.
Between this altered bastion and the North Postern is a stile which leads to a grassy area from which the outside of the fort can be viewed. Children should be warned against going onto the main road because of fast

Part of the Roman wall.

and heavy traffic. Next to the North Postern are more Second World War fortifications. Note that great care was taken to make the modern additions look as much like the ruins as possible, particularly from the air. Comparisons can be drawn with animals, birds and insects which camouflage themselves to avoid detection by their enemies.

Note on building methods: vertical cracks in the walls indicate that they were built in sections by gangs of workers. Subsequent robbing of the facing stones has allowed erosion of the joins by the weather.

Activity 2

1.
There is some doubt as to the exact location(s) of the Roman harbour(s) but it seems likely that there would have been sheltered water to the north and north-east of the fort.
Pirates would have been either killed, or taken into slavery, possibly to be sold on the continent. Keeping them to work locally might have risked betrayal and escape.

2, 3 and 4.
The sketch should be a clear outline on which measurements can be entered for use in scale drawing and modelling later. Children should be encouraged to concentrate on the shape and proportions of the gate and the building materials that have been used in its construction.

5.
Pacing may be a suitable form of measurement here, to be turned into conventional measurement on the spot if children are capable of the calculation.

6.
Self-explanatory. Can be used as a basis for calculation later if required.

7.
See Activity 1 question 7.

8.
Encourage the children to distinguish between Roman, Norman and Second World War building. Roman has distinctive bands of tiles and is more massive than Norman. Second World War building has characteristic shape and slightly different building materials.

9.
An observation task to extend information given by the teacher during completion of Activity 1.

10.
May need encouragement from an adult helper. Try to involve every member of the group.

11.
A quiet task for children to do alone. Some might like to write a poem.

Activity 3

1.
An observation task. Draw attention to differences between Roman and twentieth century building materials.

2.
At an angle.

3.
Two.

4.
Two defenders could fight one attacker (in theory anyway!)

5.
Yes. The bastion with the Norman alteration overlooked this area.

6.
As long as there were enough defenders, the North Postern would not be an easy entrance for attackers. In quieter times, spies and messengers might come and go quietly by this gate.

7.
About 3.6m.

8.
Self-explanatory.

9.
Extra height and a window.

10.
Local people for building barns and houses. Nicely shaped blocks of stone were particularly valuable for corners of flint buildings and foundations of wooden ones.

11 and 12.
See answers to Activity 2.

Activity 4

1.
Ballistas (giant crossbows)

2 and 3.
Seaward bastion has been more subject to erosion from south-westerly storms.

4.
Pace or measure (9m).

5.
Part of one of the stone jambs of the Norman gate is still attached to the taller bastion.

6 and 7.
A clear outline is needed on which measurements can be entered for later use in scale drawing. Concentrate on shape, proportions and building materials.

8.
Although care has been taken to make the pill-box look as Roman as possible, the colour of the modern concrete is slightly darker and modern 'frogged' bricks have been used in an attempt to deceive enemy aircraft into thinking that this was Roman, tile-banded masonry.

9 and 10.
See Activity 2.

Medieval Castle

Activity 1

This sheet can be discussed and worked through by the class as a whole. It is assumed that children will be familiar with common terms such as the following:

Bastion. A Roman tower (solid all through).

Fort. The Roman fortification.

Castle. The medieval fortification.

Moat. A wide, deep ditch.

Palisade. A strong, high fence. In this case inside the moat or ditch.

Bailey. The area inside the fortification.

The Gatehouse

Pill-box. A small fortified room. In this case refers to the twentieth century fortifications.

1. Simple measurement.
2. A bridge, possibly one that could be raised.
3. Explain that the sea was where the flat land is now. The line of the original ditch and palisade which cut off the end of the Roman fort to make the Norman castle is assumed to be that of the south/north arm of the moat extended along the present day ditch. The east/west arm of the moat is medieval.

4. Self explanatory.
5. This tower is believed to have been added to in Norman times. A filled in Norman window is just visible from the west. There is also a Second World War addition. Beam slots held beams for a floor or ceiling.
6. Possibly an observation point.
7. Traffic is very dangerous on this sharp bend. Children should not be allowed out of the castle unsupervised. The herring bone pattern of repairs is typically Norman.

Activity 2

The questions on this sheet can all be answered from the outside of the medieval castle. Children can be divided into groups, each group to tackle one section and report to the full class, either on-site or later in the classroom. Information gained can be used as a basis for follow-up work in modelling, mathematics, etc.

1. The Moat. Even a dry moat can be a good defence as it makes it more difficult to launch a large-scale attack, exhausts the soldiers climbing down and up the slopes and battering rams and siege towers are more difficult to use. A water-filled moat adds to these hazards. Even if the water can be let out by the enemy, mud remains. The later part of the moat(E/W) is very straight.

2. Estimation can be arrived at in many ways, e.g. how many people each 1.8m high standing on each other's shoulders (allow 1.5m per person to calculate height of object.) Round towers resist collapse by undermining better than square ones, They are wider at the bottom for the same reason. Walls were crenellated but these battlements have perished. Notice building materials.

3. The Gatehouse. The Gateway and the towers are all part of the same structure. The Towers, however, are investigated as part of Activity Sheet No.4 Living in the Castle.

Portcullis grooves stopped just above ground level to allow for the lower spikes of the portcullis. There would have been a mechanism in the upper part of the towers to work the drawbridge and another gate inside the passage so that attackers who got through the first gate could be fired upon through the murder hole.

Activity 3

Children will need to go inside the castle in order to answer these questions. It is suggested that a class should be split into three groups to answer question 1, each group to write down the information gained from one tower only. However, all should be encouraged to explore the other towers. The class can meet together later to exchange information and fill in the boxes they missed. Questions 2 to 9 can be tackled by pairs of children working together. Each pair will need a ruler and a measuring tape or other measuring device. It will probably avoid congestion if the pairs in each group tackle the questions in a different order. It is hoped that children will have practised measuring height by the ruler method and estimating height before they come to Pevensey. If not, some help will be needed. An easy method of estimating height is to stand one child of known height against the object to be measured and estimate how many would be needed to reach to the top, then multiply the two figures.

1. Observation and recording in box diagram. Children might be encouraged to speculate as to why there was ornamental stone carving only in the NW tower (we have no information on that point!) The twentieth century alterations in the other two towers were made to provide quarters for the garrison.
4. The line of the walkway can most clearly be seen where it crosses the ruined towers.
5. Self-explanatory.
6. The sea would have covered all of the flat land. The Postern Gate might have been entered from the harbour which would have been quicker than coming through the main gates. In a siege, it could have been used as a gate from which to escape, or to let out troops to harass the enemy.
7. The eastern wall of the keep was originally built into the east wall of the Roman fort. Both have now fallen. There is not room here to use the ruler method for measuring height.
8. High up on the inside of the southern wall of the keep is evidence of another floor.
9. Contrast the thickness of the walls of the keep with those of the medieval curtain wall. Whilst in this area, notice that there are remains from Roman times (the tile-banded tower), the medieval remains and also look for twentieth century fortifications at the foot of the keep.

Activity 4

Children will need to be inside the castle to answer these questions. As the remains of living quarters are so slight, they will need to be reminded of information learned in their preliminary lessons and encouraged to relate this to the clues they find.

1. There are remains of three chimneys on the north wall, although the one nearest to the east is very slight. There are two between the NW tower and the Barbican gateway, one between the gateway and the S tower and one between the S tower and the postern. Encourage speculation as to which fireplaces belong to the Hall, the Queens rooms and the kitchen.
2. In a nineteenth century excavation, 6 people were found buried in the chapel, mostly 1.5m below the floor. Three of them were children.
3. The buildings were built of timber, lath and plaster which have rotted away; the buildings have been deliberately destroyed.
4. Possibly the one between the gatehouse and the S tower. The one by the postern is more likely to have been in a guardroom. The Queen's chambers adjoined the chapel so were probably against the west wall, the Great Hall and its adjoining rooms on the north wall.
5. Encourage them to reason this one out. Where was the most convenient place? Might they have been against a wall, or freestanding?
6. Self-explanatory.
7. Evidence suggest the room(s) were for prisoners. Note the fireplace and evidence of more than one floor to the tower.
8. Self-explanatory.
9. Slots for door to be barred from outside.
10. Self-explanatory.

Glossary

Meanings given in this glossary are those which the words have in the context of this pack.

Bastion. A Roman tower.
Castleward. Garrison duty. A feudal service in return for land.
Castelwerke. Probably building operations at the castle. A feudal service owed in return for land. Constable. Captain of the royal estate of Pevensey, who had custody of the castle and prisoners and limited judicial authority.
Court Roll. The record of a Court's activities.
Curtain walls. The outside walls of the Castle.
Ditch. Moat.
Fee or fief. A unit of land charged with the provision of one knight for the lord's or the king's service.

An estate might consist of several fees.
Feudal Host. An army consisting of those who owed feudal service to the king and his tenants-in-chief, which assembled to support the king in wartime.
Feudalism. Social organization based on holding land from a superior on specified terms of service.
Heckage. One of the services rendered in exchange for land, consisting of the maintenance of hedges or fences as required. Probably referred to the maintenance of the paling fence of the castle.
Hide. An area of land used as a tax assessment.
Hundred. An administrative sub-division of a county.
Pipe or tun of wine. Large cask of wine.
Rape. There were five Rapes, sub-divisions of Sussex.
Pevensey was one of them. Each has a major castle and was controlled by a tenant-in-chief in medieval times.
Scutage. Money payment in lieu of personal military service. More usual from Henry II's reign onwards.
Sheriff or shire reeve. The king's deputy in the county.
Tenant in chief. One who held a large amount of land directly from the Crown.

English Heritage

The visit

Plan your visit well, allowing enough time for a general look around and for the activities you have chosen. Since Pevensey contains other centres of interest, decide whether you wish to stay for a whole day at the castle or see other places as well. To do justice to the castle and to the children at least a morning or afternoon is required, but the various activities can fill a whole day. A great deal of the castle is open to the elements, so warm and waterproof clothing may be necessary. Stonework and lawns can get slippery, so sensible footwear is needed at all times of the year.

It is compulsory to have a ratio of at least one adult to every fifteen children and children must be supervised throughout the visit.

Booking a visit

Free educational visits
Pevensey Castle is in the care of English Heritage. It may be visited free of charge by parties of schoolchildren or students, provided that arrangements are made in advance. Applications must be made to the Area Office, address below, at least a fortnight before the proposed visit. A free admission permit also entitles the teacher to make a free visit beforehand in preparation.

How to get there
The castle is situated in the town centre of Pevensey, on the A259 between Westham and Pevensey, and is served by frequent buses from Eastbourne and Hastings. Ordnance Survey map 199; ref TQ 645048 Parking: set down and pick up points, but nearest coach and minibus parking 200 metres from the site.

Facilities
There are toilets in the car park and a sales kiosk at the castle. Refreshments are available nearby. Much of the castle is accessible to wheelchairs, except for the towers.

Useful addresses
To apply for free admission:
   English Heritage Area Office
   Spur 17, Government Buildings
   Hawkenbury
   Tunbridge Wells
   TN2 5AQ
   Tel. 0892-548166

For information on castle opening times etc:
   The Head Custodian
   Pevensey Castle
   Pevensey
   East Sussex
   BN24 5JP
   Tel. 0323-762604

Our free booklet **Information for Teachers,** contains a list of all our sites together with many practical ideas for getting the most out of school visits, and our booking form. Our catalogue **Resources** is also available on request. For copies of the above, further details of our teachers' courses and any other information about our Education Service please contact:
   English Heritage
   Education Service
   Keysign House
   429 Oxford Street
   London W1R 2HD
   071-973 3442/3
   Fax 071-973 3430

Bibliography

Books for teachers

D F Renn, **Pevensey Castle,** English Heritage, 1970, ISBN 0-11-670060-2. The detailed guide book.

The following are archaeological reports with plans and drawings of finds from various excavations:

J P Bushe-Fox, **Journal of Roman Studies,** 1932, xxii, page 60f.

L Salzman, **Sussex Archaeological Collections,** 1907, 51 (page 99f) and 52 (page 83f).

S E Winbolt, **Victoria County History: Sussex,** III, pages 5-6.

Roman

David Breeze, **Roman Forts in Britain,** Shire Publications, 1983, ISBN 0-85263-654-7. Good, short, introduction to Roman forts.

A S Edmonde Cleary, **The Ending of Roman Britain,** Batsford, 1989, ISBN 0-7134-5275-7. Up-to-date summary of mid-fourth century Britain.

Anne Johnson, **Roman Forts,** A & C Black, 1983, ISBN 0-7136-2223-7. The authoritative study with many illustrations of building types.

Stephen Johnson, **The Roman Forts of the Saxon Shore,** Elek, 1979, ISBN 0-236-401-653. The definitive study with sections on Pevensey Castle.

Stephen Johnson, **Later Roman Britain,** Routledge & Kegan Paul, 1980, ISBN 0-586-08372-3. Provides the setting for the decline of Roman Britain.

Barri Jones and David Mattingley, **An Atlas of Roman Britain,** Blackwell, 1990, ISBN 0-631-13791-2. Excellent map and photo references for the development and decline of Roman Britain.

T W Potter, **Roman Britain,** British Museum Publications, 1983, ISBN 0-7141-2023-5. Good introduction with many photographs.

John Wacher, **The Roman Empire,** Dent, 1987, ISBN 0-460-04331-5. Provides context of the British province in a large empire.

Roger Wilson, **Roman Forts,** Bergstrom & Boyle, 1980, ISBN 0-903767-30-9. Excellent summary with many good plans, drawings and photographs.

Castles in General

R Allen Brown, **Castles, a History and Guide,** New Orchard Editions, 1980, ISBN 1-85078-013-2. Beautifully illustrated and wide ranging.

R Allen Brown, **Castles, Shire Archaeology,** 1985, ISBN 0-85263-653-9. A good introduction to British castles.

English Heritage

R Allen Brown, **English Castle,** Batsford 1976. ISBN 0-90748-606-1 — standard work on the origins and development of castle design.

D J Cathcart King, **The Castle in England and Wales,** Croon Helm, 1988, ISBN 0-7099-4829-8. For the enthusiast.

D Renn, John Baker, **Norman Castles in Britain,** 1968, ISBN 0-212-99818-8.

A Sorrel, **British Castle,** Batsford, 1973, 0-713-41119-8 — good reconstruction pictures.

M V Thompson, **The Decline of the Castle,** Cambridge University Press, 1987, ISBN 0-521-32194-8.

Medieval Life

F Andrews, **The Medieval Builder,** E P, 1976. ISBN 0-85409-962-X — detailed study of different building crafts and individual craftsmen.

A Borg, **Arms & Armour in Britain,** HMSO, 1979, ISBN 0-11-670576-0 — well illustrated introduction to medieval weapons.

J & F Giles, **Life in a Medieval Castle,** Abelard, 1975, ISBN 0-200-72416-9 — everyday life of the people who lived in the castles.

M Girouard, **Life in the English Country House,** Yale 1978, ISBN 0-300-02273-5 includes a useful account of the castle as a home.

Colin Platt, **Medieval England,** Routledge & Kegan Paul, 1978, ISBN 0-7100-8815-9.

Books for children

A wide range of books is available. The list below gives some good examples.

Roman

Peter Connolly, **The Roman Army,** Macdonald, 1975, ISBN 0-356-05110-2, Excellent drawings of soldiers, weapons, armour and battles.

Mike Corbishley, **The Roman World,** Kingfisher, 1986, ISBN 0-86272-218-7. Good introduction with many reconstruction drawings.

Mike Corbishley, **Ancient Rome: cultural atlas for young people.** Facts on File, 1989, ISBN 0-8160-1970-3. Valuable introduction with reconstruction drawings and section on Roman Britain.

Miranda Green, **Roman Archaeology,** Longman, 1963, ISBN 0-582-20165-9. Good introduction to archaeological techniques using Roman examples.

Simon James, **Ancient Rome,** Dorling Kindersley, 1990, ISBN 0-86318-445-6. One of the Eyewitness Guides.

Castles

Althea, **Castle Life,** Cambridge University Press, 1977, ISBN 0-521-271557. For younger children.

Susan Baker, **Castles,** Macdonald, 1987, ISBN 0-3561-0-51442-X.

Brian Davison, **Looking at a Castle,** Kingfisher, 1987, ISBN 0-86272-251-9. Although written for the younger child, its illustrations are useful to older children.

Brian Davison, **The New Observers Book of Castles,** Frederick Warne, 1988, ISBN 0-7232-3339-X. A classic handbook.

Marie Farre, **Long Ago in a Castle,** Moonlight Publications, 1986, ISBN 0-85103-008-5. Full of medieval illuminated manuscript illustrations.

Hugh Gregor, **Castles: a guide for young people,** HMSO, 1977, ISBN 0-11-671085-3.

Judy Hindley, **Knights and Castles,** Time Traveller Books, Usborne, 1976, ISBN 0-860020-067-1.

David Macaulay, **Castles,** Collins, 1977, ISBN 0-00-195128-9. A brilliantly illustrated story of a Welsh castle.

Vanessa Miles, **Castles and Dungeons,** Transworld, 1985, ISBN 0-552-542-652. Lots of fun and unusual facts.

Jonathan Rutland, **Knights and Castles,** Kingfisher, 1978, ISBN 0-86272-260-8.

David Woodlander, **Castles,** Black, 1983, ISBN 0-71362-271-7.

Jenny Vaughan, **Castles,** Franklin Watts, 1984, ISBN 0-86313-080-1.

Life in Medieval Times

Mike Corbishley, **The Middle Ages: Cultural Atlas for Young People**, Facts on File, 1990, ISBN 0-8160-1973-8.

Penelope Davies, **Growing Up in the Middle Ages**, Wayland, 1972, ISBN 0-85340-174-8.

Peter Lane, **Visual Sources: Norman England**, Batsford, 1980, ISBN 0-7134-33-56.

Robin May, **William the Conqueror and the Normans**, Wayland, 1984, ISBN 0-85078-470-0.

Ray Mitchell and Geoff Middleton, **Norman and Medieval Britain**, Longman, 1988, ISBN 0-582-18315-4.

Greg Thie, **Living in the past — The Middle Ages**, Blackwell, 1988, ISBN 0-631-91140-5.

Frances Wilkins, **Growing Up During the Norman Conquest**, Batsford, 1980, ISBN 0-7134-3360-4.

Martin Windrow, **Medieval Knight**, Franklin Watts, 1985, ISBN 0-86313-180-8.

Fiction

Arthur Conan Doyle, **Sir Nigel**, Pan 1976, ISBN 3-302-4711-5.

Roger Lancelyn Green, **The Adventures of Robin Hood**, Puffin, ISBN 0-140-35034-9.

W O Hassall, **They Saw it Happen 55BC-1485AD**, Blackwell, 1959, ISBN 0631052801 — good extracts from original sources.

Mary Ray, **Spring Tide,** Faber, 1969, ISBN 0-571-11331-1. Story set in the Roman garrison town of Cardiff in the late Roman period.

Sir Walter Scott, **Ivanhoe**, Dent, 1983, ISBN 0-460-10016-5.

R C Sherriff, **Siege of Swayne's Castle**, Armada, 1975, ISBN 0-006-71056-5.

George Shipway, **Knight in Anarchy**, Peter Davis, 1969, ISBN 0-432-14751-9.

Rosemary Sutcliff, **Knight's Fee**, Oxford University Press, 1974, ISBN 0-19-277066-7.

Geoffrey Trease, **Bows against the Barons**, University of London Press, 1966, ISBN 0-340-04043-2.

Geoffrey Trease, **Baron's Hostage**, Knight, 1974, ISBN 0-340-17938-4.

Henry Treece, **The eagles have flown,** Bodley Head/Knight, 1954, ISBN 0-340-03995-7. Britain in the fifth century AD.

Henry Treece, **The Children's Crusade**, Puffin, ISBN 014030414X.

Ronald Welch, **Bowman of Crecy**, Oxford University Press, 1973, ISBN 0-19-271256-X.

Archaeological Approaches

The Council for British Archaeology produces a series: **Archaeology for Schools**, (ISBN 0262 897X) of which **Upstanding Archaeology**, **Archaeology in the Classroom**, and **Archaeology in Primary Schools** are particularly useful. They are available from the CBA, 112 Kennington Road, London, SE11 6RE.

Drama and Role Play

John Fairclough and Patrick Redsell, **Living History, Reconstructing the Past with Children**, English Heritage, 1985, ISBN 1-85074-073-9.

Food and Cooking

Maggie Black, **Food and Cooking in Medieval Britain**, English Heritage, 1985, ISBN 1-850-74-081-1X.

Peter Briars, **Food and Cooking in Sixteenth Century Britain**, English Heritage, 1985. ISBN 1-85074-082-8.

Gill Corbishley, **Ration Book Recipes Some Food Facts 1939-1954,** English Heritage, 1990.
ISBN 1-85074-288-X.
A summary of facts about food rationing with recipes. Special section outlines possible National Curriculum Studies in various core subjects.

Jane Renfrew, **Food and Cooking in Roman Britain,** English Heritage, 1985, ISBN 1-85074-080-1.

These publications are available from English Heritage, PO Box 229, Northampton NN6 9RY.

English Heritage Videos

Available on free loan or purchase from English Heritage, PO Box 229, Northampton NN6 9RY.

Looking at a Castle, for age 11-13; 14 minutes; 1980.

The Norman Conquest for England, for aged 11-16; 15 minutes; 1982.

Living History, for teacher training; 20 minutes; 1986.

Archaeological Detectives
This series aims to show children how enjoyable detective observation of historical evidence can be, and to help them record and reach conclusions about the buildings and objects of the past.

The Archaeological Detectives — Investigating on site, for age range 9-13; 20 minutes; 1989.

Clues Challenge, for age 9-13; 14 minutes; 1990.

Bits and Bodies, age range 9-13; 33 minutes; 1990.

Slides and Software

Castles (A114): a set of 12 slides showing the development of castles.

Fletcher's Castle (Fernleaf). Castle building computer simulation.

Both distributed by the Slide Centre, Ilton, Ilminster, Somerset, TA19 9HS. Tel. 0460 57151.

Posters

A set of nine full colour photographic posters showing the development of castles and later fortifications can be purchased from English Heritage, PO Box 229, Northampton NN6 9RY.

OPPOSITE ABOVE: The castle as it was early in the twentieth century.
OPPOSITE BELOW: The castle in 1990.

36